Understanding Jacques Ellul

Understanding Jacques Ellul

Jeffrey P. Greenman
Read Mercer Schuchardt
Noah J. Toly

CASCADE *Books* • Eugene, Oregon

UNDERSTANDING JACQUES ELLUL

Copyright © 2012 Jeffrey P. Greenman, Read Mercer Schuchardt, and Noah J. Toly. All rights reserved. Except for brief quotations in critical publications or reviews, no part of this book may be reproduced in any manner without prior written permission from the publisher. Write: Permissions. Wipf and Stock Publishers, 199 W. 8th Ave., Suite 3, Eugene, OR 97401.

Cascade Books
An Imprint of Wipf and Stock Publishers
199 W. 8th Ave., Suite 3
Eugene, OR 97401

www.wipfandstock.com

ISBN 13: 978-1-61097-431-8

Cataloguing-in-Publication Data

Greenman, Jeffrey P.

    Understanding Jacques Ellul / Jeffrey P. Greenman, Read Mercer Schuchardt, and Noah J. Toly.

    xvi + 174 p.; 23 cm—Includes bibliographical references and index(es).

    ISBN: 978-1-61097-431-8

    1. Ellul, Jacques—Criticism and interpretation. I. Schuchardt, Read Mercer. II. Toly, Noah. III. Title.

BX4827.E5 G74 2012

Manufactured in the USA.

Contents

Acknowledgments | vii
Introduction | ix

CHAPTER 1 Ellul's Life and Thought | 1
CHAPTER 2 Technology and Technique | 19
CHAPTER 3 Communication: Media, Propaganda, and the Word | 38
CHAPTER 4 The City and Urbanism | 60
CHAPTER 5 Politics and Economics | 81
CHAPTER 6 Scripture | 98
CHAPTER 7 Ethics | 121
CHAPTER 8 Ellul as a Christian Scholar | 145

Key Events in the Life of Jacques Ellul | 161

Bibliography | 163
Index | 171

Acknowledgments

As faculty members at Wheaton College, we are grateful to our Provost, Stan Jones, and our academic deans, Jill Baumgaertner, Dorothy Chappell, and Michael Wilder, for their support and encouragement for our teaching and scholarship related to Jacques Ellul. David Malone and David Gill provided valuable input at key stages of our research and writing. In addition, we want to acknowledge the excellent assistance provided by Steve Pardue, whose careful editorial work with our manuscript made this book possible.

Introduction

Upon this gifted age, in its dark hour,
Rains from the sky a meteoric shower
Of facts . . . they lie unquestioned, uncombined.
Wisdom enough to leech us of our ill
Is daily spun, but there exists no loom
To weave it into fabric.[1]

JACQUES ELLUL IS ONE of the looms of the last one hundred years. If you are looking for a single-source "guide for the perplexed" to understand what just happened in the twentieth century, what it means, and what can be done about it, he is one of a handful of individuals whose writings should be studied. He did not know everything, and he did not interpret everything accurately, but he was one of the world's last great polymaths and one of the most salient Christian thinkers of his era. With a goal of offering a comprehensive appraisal of the modern world, and of the place of Christian faith in it, he wrote over fifty books and a thousand articles. He addressed almost every major facet and institution of modern society and many more from previous ages. He engaged his material with simplicity, sincerity, courage, and a passion that few have matched. As he wrote in the introduction to one of his most widely acclaimed books,

> I try to do here the same thing I do in all my books: face, alone, this world I live in, try to understand it, and confront it with another reality I live in, but which is utterly unverifiable. Taking my place at the level of the simplest of daily experiences, I make my way without critical weapons. Not as a scientist, but as an ordinary

---

1. Edna St. Vincent Millay, from *Huntsman, What Quarry?*, cited in Postman, "Science and the Story We Need," 29.

Introduction

person, without scientific pretensions, talking about what we all experience. I feel, listen, and look.[2]

His remarkably broad field of vision, his clarity of focus, and his boldly prophetic voice make his work worth reading and considering, rereading and discussing.

Ellul's thinking is simultaneously quite dark and relentlessly hopeful, revealing a powerful tension that is both shocking and discomforting to those who think they know Ellul by virtue of having followed only one or two threads of his complex oeuvre. This book offers an analysis and assessment of the most important themes in Ellul's work. It aims to orient readers in such a way as to invite further exploration. Put simply, if Ellul is one of the few remarkably good entry points for understanding the facts, figures, forces, and consequences of the last century, then this book aims to be the entry point for understanding Ellul. If Ellul offers themes and threads by which one might understand late modern society, we hope to offer themes and threads by which one might understand and more fruitfully appropriate Ellul.

As we have taught university-level courses on Ellul, we have realized the need for this book, since there is no single-volume introduction to his ideas and their significance. Because there seems to be the sociological Ellul and the theological Ellul, the technological Ellul and the ethical Ellul, the personal Ellul and the political Ellul—and a few more Elluls in between—we have endeavored to shine what collective, cross-disciplinary understanding we have on his life and work in order to bring a fuller, more robust, and more realistic Ellul into the light. It is our hope that you will find here a voice worth listening to, a mind worth engaging, and a man for our times.

---

2. Ellul, *Humiliation of the Word*, 1.

CHAPTER 1

Ellul's Life and Thought

ALTHOUGH JACQUES ELLUL WROTE over fifty books and one thousand articles during his career, his life involved much more than a professor's typical labors of lecturing and writing.[1] Andrew Goddard has aptly commented that "Ellul's life and his thought are intricately interwoven. He wrote out of what he lived and he lived out what he wrote."[2] This chapter aims to set the stage for understanding Ellul's thought by locating his writings in the context of his life.

Early Years and Education

Jacques César Ellul was born on January 6, 1912, in Bordeaux, France.[3] He spent almost his entire life in the southwest region of his home country, some six hundred kilometers removed from Paris. He was the only child of Joseph and Martha Ellul. Joseph Ellul was an Austrian subject of Serbian-Italian heritage, and Martha Ellul was French from Portuguese-Jewish

---

1. The most complete record of Ellul's writings is found in Hanks, *Annotated Bibliography*.
2. Goddard, *Living the Word*, 2.
3. No one has yet written a comprehensive biography of Ellul. He apparently wrote an extensive autobiography that has not been made public. The main sources for his life are extensive interviews he gave on various occasions, which have been collected into individual volumes. See Garrigou-Lagrange, *In Season*; Ellul, *Perspectives*; Ellul, *Ellul on Religion, Technology, and Politics*. In addition, there is a fifty-four-minute film titled *The Betrayal by Technology: A Portrait of Jacques Ellul* made by Jan van Boekel, based on interviews filmed in 1990. See also Goddard, "Obituary."

ancestry. Ellul was "what people call a *métèque*, a product of the melting pot,"[4] as he recalled in reflection upon his mixed heritage. *Métèque* is a derogatory term in France for Mediterranean foreigners, suggesting Ellul's identity as an outsider to the mainstream of French society. Although both of his parents had been raised in aristocratic families, the Ellul family lived in poverty. His mother was a painter and teacher of art lessons. His father was a businessman who struggled through the economic catastrophe of the Depression, often without steady work. Ellul said: "One of the most important, most decisive elements in my life was that I grew up in a rather poor family. I experienced true poverty in every way, and I know very well the life of a family in a wretched milieu, with all the educational problems that this involves and the difficulties of having to work while still very young. I had to make my living from the age of fifteen, and I pursued all my studies while earning my own and sometimes my family's livelihood."[5]

Despite this, Ellul recalled a happy childhood, spending time on the docks at the port of Bordeaux and visiting the *Jardin Public* with its trees, ponds, and fountains. His only "bad memory" was "harassment in high school because I was the smallest in the class—and the best student."[6] He writes of loving parents: "I lived with two parents who loved me very much, but in completely different ways. My father was very distant . . . my mother was very close to me, though extremely reserved."[7] Concerning his religious upbringing, Ellul stated that he "really did not have any at all." His father was "a skeptic, a Voltairian" in outlook, and therefore quite critical of religion. "He didn't forbid that I receive any kind of Christian education, but nothing was done in that direction."[8] His mother was a Protestant whom Ellul describes as "deeply religious" but who kept her faith to herself: "she never spoke to me about it; she never told me anything."[9] Despite this situation, as a child he read the Bible by himself. Ellul was not raised in "a Christian atmosphere" but later experienced a dramatic Christian conversion.

Despite the family's poverty, when Ellul graduated from high school, his mother insisted that he begin university rather than get a job immediately. His father overruled Ellul's desire for a career as a naval officer and

4. Garrigou-Lagrange, *In Season*, 4–5.
5. Ellul, *Perspectives*, 1.
6. Garrigou-Lagrange, *In Season*, 7.
7. Ellul, *Perspectives*, 2.
8. Garrigou-Lagrange, *In Season*, 13.
9. Ellul, *Perspectives*, 2.

steered him toward law.[10] This resonated for pragmatic reasons; according to Ellul, law "was a subject that seemed to lead to a profession, and the study of it was relatively short. Those were frankly the only reasons I had for choosing it."[11] He began his studies in law at the University of Bordeaux in 1929, the year of the worldwide economic crash. He completed his *licence en droit* in 1931 and his *licence libre et lettres* in 1932; after his mandatory military service during 1934–35, he completed his doctoral thesis in 1936 on an ancient Roman legal institution, the *mancipium* (the right of father to sell children). During 1937, he taught at Montpellier and then in 1938 took a position at Strasbourg University.

Turning Points

Early in his law studies there were two decisive events—reading Karl Marx and becoming a Christian.[12] Of his conversion, Ellul said, "I was alone in the house busy translating Faust when suddenly, and I have no doubts on this at all, I knew myself to be in the presence of something so astounding, so overwhelming that entered me to the very centre of my being. That's all I can tell you. I was so moved that I left the room in a stunned state. In the courtyard there was a bicycle lying around. I jumped on it and fled."[13] He explained:

> I was converted—not by someone, nor can I say I converted myself. It is a very personal story, but I will say it was a very brutal and very sudden conversion.... From that moment on, I lived through the conflict and contradiction between what became the center of my life—this faith, this reference to the Bible, which I henceforth read from a different perspective—and what I knew of Marx and did not wish to abandon. For I did not see why I should have to give up the things that Marx said about society and explained about economy and injustice in the world. I saw no reason to reject them just because I was now a Christian.[14]

---

10. Garrigou-Lagrange, *In Season*, 19. It should be noted that the study of law in early twentieth-century France was the study of social institutions, rather than preparation for the practice of law or a career as an attorney.

11. Ellul, *Perspectives*, 4.

12. Ellul, *Ellul on Religion, Technology, and Politics*, 55.

13. Ibid., 52.

14. Ellul, *Perspectives*, 11–12.

> One of the most important elements of his conversion was that Ellul encountered the Bible in a new way. He recalled that reading the eighth chapter of Paul's letter to the Romans was "a watershed in my life. In fact, it was such a totally decisive experience that it became one of the steps in my conversion. And for the first time in my life, a biblical text really became God's Word to me. . . . It became a living contemporary Word, which I could no longer question, which was beyond all discussion. And that Word then became the point of departure for all my reflection in the faith."[15]

Regarding his encounter with Marx, Ellul explained:

> In 1930, I discovered Marx. I read *Das Kapital* and I felt I understood everything. I felt that at last I knew why my father was out of work, at last I knew why we were destitute. For a boy of seventeen, perhaps eighteen, it was an astonishing revelation about the society he lived in. It also illuminated the working-class condition I had plunged into and those dealings at the port of Bordeaux . . . Thus, for me, Marx was an astonishing discovery of the reality of this world . . . I plunged into Marx's thinking with an incredible joy: I had finally found *the* explanation . . . Marx provided an intellectual formulation of what, for me, had to come from experience, from life, from concrete reality.[16]

As his own writings unfolded, Ellul's viewpoint imitated Marx's at least in its search for a comprehensive explanation of the social realities of the modern world. In this sense, Marx's work was an inspiration and model. Ellul commented: "As I became more and more familiar with Marxist thought, I discovered that his was not only an economic system, not only the exposure of the mechanics of capitalism. It was a total vision of the human race, society, and history. And since I did not follow any creed, religion, or philosophy . . . I was bound to find something extremely satisfying in Marx."[17] In an important early essay, Ellul argued that a "new Karl Marx" was needed. He wrote, "Marx was the only man of his time who grasped the totality of the social, political, and economic problems in their reality and posed correctly the questions [facing] the civilization of the nineteenth century."[18] Writing in 1947, Ellul commented that "what seems absolutely

---

15. Ellul, "How I Discovered Hope," 28.
16. Ellul, *Perspectives*, 4–6.
17. Ibid., 5.
18. Ellul, "New Karl Marx," 38.

necessary today is to do again precisely the same work that Karl Marx did a hundred years ago."[19]

Ellul was influenced by Marx's understanding of a "materialist conception of history," according to which human history is shaped decisively by material factors more than changes of ideas. Ellul realized that in the twentieth century, changes in technology were producing profound changes in social organization. Ellul was not uncritical of Marx on certain key points, but was particularly indebted to Marx for pointing him toward the issue of social revolution as a major concern; for increasing his awareness of economic realities and interests in the analysis of any ideology or theory; and for inspiring his "decision to side with the poor . . . with people who are alienated at all levels." It was because of Marx that he "sided with the excluded, sided with the unfit, sided with those on the fringes."[20] It should be noted that Ellul stated, "In the religious area . . . Marx had no influence at all. . . . I was not particularly touched by his arguments about religion and God."[21]

Despite Ellul's admiration for Marx, he realized that "Marx did not have answers for everything. . . . In regard to life itself, a certain number of problems were still open. It was here that the Bible gave me more, establishing itself in my life on a different level than Marx's explanations about society. In the Bible, I was led to discover an entire world that was very new to me . . . a new world when I compared it with the realities of life and of my life and experience."[22]

Friendships and Family

Ellul stated that "two writings—Marx and the Gospel—and then two people—Jean Bosc and Bernard Charbonneau—formed my personality."[23] Ellul described himself as a "man of friendships" with "some of the most astonishing and extraordinary friends."[24] In particular, two close friends, Charbonneau (1910–1996) and Bosc (1910–1969), played key roles in Ellul's life and intellectual development. Ellul met Charbonneau in high

19. Ellul, *Sources and Trajectories*, 40.
20. Ellul, *Perspectives*, 9–10.
21. Ibid., 10.
22. Ibid., 11.
23. Garrigou-Lagrange, *In Season*, 27.
24. Ibid., 23.

school and they remained in close contact throughout their lives. Charbonneau was a non-Christian philosopher, social critic, and environmentalist, whom Ellul considered "one of the rare geniuses of our time."[25] Ellul always credited Charbonneau with having "a decisive influence on my choice of direction in research and thought"; Charbonneau, he said, taught him "how to 'think.' But he also taught me to see the reality of society, instead of looking only into my books. He taught me to consider actively the social fact, 'what is really happening'—to analyze, to criticize, to understand it."[26] Charbonneau's critical importance for Ellul was directing him toward research on the subject of technique, which would become the main focus of Ellul's sociological works.

Bosc, a Reformed Church pastor, introduced Ellul and many others in France to the theology of Karl Barth. Bosc served as director of the French biweekly journal *Foi & Vie: La Revue de Culture Protestante* (*Faith & Life: The Protestant Review of Culture*) between 1957 and 1969. Ellul succeeded him in this role, serving between 1969 and 1986, and wrote approximately seventy articles for the journal. Ellul had the highest praise for Bosc as an exemplary Christian whose presence was "like the presence of God's love."[27]

Finally, Ellul described meeting his wife, Yvette, as "the most decisive turning point" in his life.[28] They married in 1937. Together they had four children: Jean, Simon, Yves, and Dominique. He credited Yvette as the one who "helped me learn to live . . . she also taught me to listen."[29] It was his relationship with Yvette that kept Ellul from traveling to Spain in order to fight in the Spanish Civil War. In one of the books of his interviews, he complained that academic and public life "is always about *me*, whereas I can't think of myself without her."[30] After her death in 1991, Ellul was distraught, grieving intensely until his own death on May 19, 1994.

Politics and Resistance

Ellul commented that "after 1933 . . . I got very deeply involved in politics." He was "part of the crowd" during the riot on February 6, 1934, in Paris,

25. Ibid., 26.
26. Ellul, "Response," 14.
27. Garrigou-Lagrange, *In Season*, 28.
28. Ibid., 31.
29. Ellul, *Ellul on Religion, Technology, and Politics*, 93.
30. Garrigou-Lagrange, *In Season*, 32.

instigated by right-wing factions that involved an attempted violent coup. In 1935, he attended a Nazi gathering in Munich "out of curiosity," and recalled that "it was fascinating to see how easily a crowd could be whipped up and welded into a single unit." In 1936, he participated in the Popular Front (an alliance of left-wing movements in the inter-war years in France). During 1937, Ellul had a "modest part" in supplying combatants in the Spanish Civil War, but he never gives much detail about his involvement.

From 1937 to 1939, Ellul served as a lecturer at Strasbourg University, a position from which he was summarily dismissed after being interrogated by police on the grounds that he had given a political talk to students from Alsace, had made "hostile" statements, and had a "foreigner" for a father. His father was arrested and imprisoned. Ellul last saw him in prison, where he died in 1942, during the German occupation of the country.

During the occupation, Ellul was "forced to join the Resistance. It was necessity, not virtue."[31] Apparently, since his wife was born in Holland and had a British passport, she was slated to be arrested. They relocated for four years to a "free zone" in the village of Martres, some fifty kilometers outside Bordeaux. To support his family during this time, Ellul became a farmer, tending sheep and growing potatoes. Ellul harvested his first ton of potatoes as he was receiving his *agrégation* (the qualifying exam for university teaching) in Roman Law in 1943. In this period, Ellul was assisting Jews to escape the Holocaust by helping them get to the free French zone: "I found false papers for them. I also organized local Resistance groups to serve as links to the marquis, the guerrilla soldiers in the outlying areas." Ellul recalled that he was "able to provide a whole series of people with forged identity cards or forged ration books."[32] For his efforts, Ellul was awarded the designation "Righteous Among the Nations" in 2001 by Yad Vashem, the Holocaust museum in Jerusalem.

At the close of the war, Ellul briefly served as a member of the Bordeaux city administration (October 1944–April 1945), responsible for public works and commerce. This experience was not a positive one. He commented: "Some of my books, for instance, *The Political Illusion*, derive in part from my experience in the political milieu—from politicians' inability to really change the world they live in, the enormous influence of administrative bodies. The politician is powerless against government

---

31. Ellul, *Perspectives*, 17.
32. Ellul, *Ellul on Religion, Technology, and Politics*, 76.

bureaucracy; society cannot be changed through political action."³³ In part because of his experience in municipal public administration, Ellul preferred small-scale, community-based, and nongovernmental social involvement. Between 1945 and 1955, he was director of a Bordeaux film club analyzing contemporary cinema.³⁴ He was president from 1958 to 1976 of an organization that worked directly with "social misfits" and street gangs. In addition to acting as liaison with police and the legal system on behalf of the youth, Ellul led Bible studies as part of the group's program. He also became active in an environmental organization dedicated to preserving the Aquitaine region on the French coast.

Philosophical Commitments and Ecclesiastical Involvement

Meanwhile, during the mid-1930s Ellul became involved in the personalist movement led by Emmanuel Mounier, author of *The Personalist Manifesto* and editor of the magazine *Espirit*. The personalist movement found its basis in the Roman Catholic tradition and sought to relate Christian faith to the critical social problems of its day. In large measure, it was a response to the worldwide economic conditions after the Wall Street crash in 1929. In general terms, the movement was critical of capitalism for its neglect of the human person in favor of economic profit. Mounier wrote: "We shall apply the term personalist to any doctrine or any civilization that affirms the primacy of the human person over material necessities and over the whole complex of implements man needs for the development of his person."³⁵ It emphasized the primacy of love with the motto "to be human is to love." Ellul recalled his involvement, saying: "We felt that a human being is a person, which means that a society must be structured purely toward developing this personhood and rejecting alienation. But on the other hand, one can be a person only if one belongs to a group, only if one belongs to a community. . . . [As for party commitments,] we belonged to no political party, we were chiefly anti-Fascist."³⁶

In terms of ecclesiastical involvement, Ellul became a lay pastor when he discovered an "abandoned Protestant church" in the village of Martres "which had no leadership." Ellul restarted it in 1943 with "regular worship

---

33. Lovekin, *Technique, Discourse, and Consciousness*, 121.
34. Goddard, *Living the Word*, 37n83.
35. Mounier, *Personalist Manifesto*, 1.
36. Ellul, *Perspectives*, 15–16.

under my direction." At first, the Elluls held services in their dining room. The church experienced rapid growth, especially of working-class families. As churchman, Ellul was also involved in the formation of the World Council of Churches (WCC) in 1945, gave lectures at the Bossey Ecumenical Institute in 1946, and served on WCC commissions. He was a major figure in preparation for the 1948 First Assembly of WCC (Amsterdam), where he presented a paper titled "The Situation in Europe."[37] However, Ellul became disillusioned with the WCC's theology, social analysis, and "bureaucratic system" in the early 1950s and ceased to be involved with the organization.

He was also a member of the National Council of the French Reformed Church (consisting of twenty members, including ten laypeople) between 1951 and 1970. This experience, too, proved disappointing. Of his involvement, he wrote, "I realized the Church would have to be changed, in order to become the leaven, a force for change in society. So I began to try to change the Reformed Church. I worked at it for fifteen years. It was a difficult job. Ultimately, I failed."[38] He later concluded that the Church was incapable of reforming itself, that it was "bogged down in the traditionalism of Christians . . . Once a movement becomes an institution, it is lost."[39]

Academic Career and Writings

From 1944 until his retirement in 1980, Jacques Ellul was Professor of the History and Sociology of Institutions in the Faculty of Law and Professor in the Institute for Political Studies. He taught Roman law, philosophy of law, and Marx and Marxism. As a legal scholar, his major work is a five-volume *opus*, *Histoire des institutions*, which treats the development of legal institutions from antiquity to the nineteenth century (it has not yet been translated into English).[40]

Ellul's varied experiences of poverty, close friendship, dramatic conversion, Marxism, politics, dislocation, resistance, government administration, interventions among juvenile delinquents, and pastoral work were major sources of reflection in his work as an author. He defined his life's work in terms of understanding the modern world. There is no mistaking his overall project as an explicitly Christian intellectual endeavor. Ellul

37. Ellul, "Situation in Europe."
38. Ellul, *Perspectives*, 19.
39. Ibid., 20.
40. Ellul, *Histoire des institutions*.

wrote: "the sociological state of the world in which we live is rather desperate, so that it is difficult for modern people, deprived of hope and given over to immediate pleasure and unconscious fear of tomorrow, to proclaim the hope of faith in Christ and in the possibility for true love. This is one major purpose that has oriented my whole life."[41] He said that he worked "without genius but with perseverance, without a transcending inspiration, but out of the conviction that my task was to unveil the realities to that man and of that time, which nobody seemed to take into account and which appeared to me to be decisive."[42] In Ellul's introduction to his book *The Humiliation of the Word*, he describes his stance as a Christian scholar: "I am not pretending to push forward scientific frontiers. Rather, I try to do here the same thing I do in all my books: face, alone, this world I live in, try to understand it, and confront it with another reality I live in, but which is utterly unverifiable."[43] In scientific terms, Ellul's faith in God is "utterly unverifiable" yet unquestionably real. From the standpoint of Ellul's theology, the modern world and biblical faith stand in a relation of tension.

Ellul did not consider himself to be a theologian, yet he wrote sophisticated theological works throughout his entire adult life. His favorite Christian thinker was the Swiss Reformed theologian Karl Barth (1886–1968), whom he preferred to John Calvin (1509–1564), the fountainhead of Reformed theology. Said Ellul: "Calvin was impossible! I spent a whole year in the early forties studying him alone. I was very unhappy with it. I cannot get into Calvin's way of reasoning."[44] Of Calvin's *Institutes*, he wrote: "I read the whole work and believe me I found it deadly boring. I have never been attracted by that kind of rigor."[45] Ellul's own temperament comes through clearly when he states: "Calvin constantly offers answers, solutions, or a construction, while Barth launches you into an adventure."[46]

Ellul regarded Barth, on the other hand, as "the second great element in my intellectual life" after Marx.[47] The significance of his discovery of Barth, himself a socialist by political persuasion, can hardly be overstated. Ellul remarked: "Barth was a signpost showing how one could get beyond

---

41. Ellul, "Response," 15.
42. Ibid., 14.
43. Ellul, *Humiliation of the Word*, 1.
44. Ellul, "Man Who Asks Hard Questions," 18.
45 Ellul, *Ellul on Religion, Technology, and Politics*, 49.
46. Ellul, *Perspectives*, 14.
47 Ibid., 14. See Bromiley, "Barth's Influence."

Ellul's Life and Thought

the stage of pure and simple contradiction between Christian faith and Karl Marx."[48] Moreover, Ellul saw his chief intellectual project as arising from Barth's work. He stated: "I had the impression that the ethical consequences of Barth's theology had never been elicited. I was not satisfied with his volumes of ethics and politics, which seemed to be based on an insufficient knowledge of the world and of politics. However, there was everything there necessary to formulate an ethic without losing any of the rediscovered truth, being totally faithful to the Scriptures, but without legalism or literalism. But this work seemed possible to me only if one conserved the groundwork laid by Barth and did not start over again."[49]

Building on a foundation of Marxist analytical inclinations and Barthian theology, Ellul was an immensely prolific writer, almost entirely on subjects outside his professional specialization in law. There are two main categories of his writings: social theoretical and theological.[50] Ellul commented: "I have always tried to prevent 'my' theology from influencing my sociological research and my comprehension of the world from distorting my reading of the Bible. These were two domains, two methods, two distinct interests. Only after the separation, one begins to perceive relationship."[51] He added: "These two elements are closely linked, because on the one hand it is only by this faith in Jesus Christ that I could do this analysis of society, and on the other hand, my analysis of the technological world demanded a more and more vigorous faith from me and an increasingly exact theological knowledge."[52] The major sociological works include *The Technological Society* (followed by *The Technological System* and *The Technological Bluff*); *Propaganda*; *The Political Illusion*; *The Humiliation of the Word*; and *The Betrayal of the West*. His main biblical, theological, and ethical works include books such as *Prayer and Modern Man*; *The Meaning of the City*; *Money and Power*; *To Will and to Do*; *The Ethics of Freedom*; and *Hope in Time of Abandonment*, as well as biblical expositions on various books of the Bible. Throughout our study of Ellul, we will engage many of

---

48. Ellul, *Perspectives*, 14.

49. Ellul, "Karl Barth and Us," 24.

50. Music aficionados will be interested to know that, according to an undocumented source, Ellul wrote to music. He listened to Mozart as he wrote his theological works and composed *The Technological Society* while listening to Bach's *Brandenburg Concertos*.

51. Ellul, "Response," 15.

52. Ellul, *Perspectives*, 75.

these volumes, attempting to forge a path toward an understanding of the corpus as a whole in the concluding chapter.

Ellul as an Outsider

A helpful way of putting Ellul's life and thought in perspective is to recognize that he was a person from the margins who brought an outsider's viewpoint to both his theory and practice. Unlike most prominent intellectuals of the twentieth century, he grew up in poverty, unfamiliar with the advantages of wealth. Despite his French citizenship, he was considered a "foreigner" in his own country due to his mixed heritage. He was from the outlying provinces, not from Paris, the center of French intellectual and social life. Ellul recounted once being asked by a journalist, "But how can you be an intellectual if you live in the provinces?"[53] He wrote only in French and did not speak English well. He never traveled to the United States, yet his popularity was and is highest in American circles. As far as politics were concerned, he "refused to join any mainstream political currents."[54]

Ellul embraced Christianity as an outsider to the faith, having been raised in a non-Christian home, and then advocated for the Christian cause with single-minded zeal. As a Christian he occupied the margins of French academic life, which was heavily secular in outlook. Within a historically Roman Catholic nation, he was a member of the tiny Reformed Protestant church. Within the church, he was a layman, not possessed of the power and privileges of a clergyman. He did relatively little writing in his academic specialty in law; most of his writings are those of a nonspecialist aimed at a nonspecialist audience. As a legal and historical scholar without formal theological training, he was never part of the mainstream in academic theology; despite his many theological books, he always disavowed any claim to be a theologian. Within the Reformed tradition, he was sharply critical of John Calvin and standard Calvinist doctrines and upheld a minority viewpoint associated with Karl Barth. As a biblical interpreter, his views are hardly conventional and often idiosyncratic. As a Christian thinker, he offered a prophetic critique of virtually all areas of life, secular and sacred, and tended to resist the status quo. Like the biblical prophets, he relentlessly challenged established orthodoxies and proposed radical alternatives, and he was often dismissed as eccentric. In all these ways, Ellul was a marginal

53. Ellul, *Ellul on Religion, Technology, and Politics*, 21.
54. Ibid.

figure. He commented that "it is obvious that I have always found myself alone and out of place."⁵⁵ This marginality, this outsider status, shaped his scholarship and activism in definitive ways, perhaps contributing to Ellul's productivity and prescience and certainly giving a distinctive character to his life and work.

The Presence of the Kingdom as Preview of Ellul's Thought

Ellul believed that his short book *The Presence of the Kingdom* provided an introduction to his entire set of writings.⁵⁶ For our purposes in setting the stage for a comprehensive exposition and analysis of Ellul's thought, we will offer a synopsis of the main themes of *Presence*, since it is so suggestive of the main directions for his later thought.

The book was first published in French in 1948 with the title, *Presence au monde modern: Problemes de la civilization post-chretienne* (literally, *Presence in the Modern World: Problems of Post-Christian Civilization*). Ellul's preface to the second edition of the book states that he wrote "on the presence of the Christian in today's world—not in the world in general, but in the world as it was."⁵⁷ The book has a preface, four chapters, and ends with a "Prologue and Conclusion." At the very end of the book, he tells the reader that it has been offered "to open the way for a work of the renewed church."⁵⁸

In the preface, Ellul explains that the work is oriented by the challenge announced by the Apostle Paul in Rom 12:2: "Do not conform to the pattern of this world, but be transformed by the renewing of your mind. Then you will be able to test and approve what God's will is—his good, pleasing and perfect will." In response to this instruction, Ellul writes, "I had to apply myself in discerning what were the foundations, the structures, the make-up of the present age: that is to say, of the twentieth century."⁵⁹ He became concerned to understand the "facts" of society on their own terms, but in "the light of Jesus Christ." As such, the book is one of a few to bring together the rudiments of Ellul's social analysis and the main themes of his theological vision of authentic Christian witness. It

---

55. Ibid.
56. Ellul, *Presence*, x.
57. Ibid., ix.
58. Ibid., 113.
59. Ibid., xi.

does this against the backdrop of an overarching concern for the church's conformity to the world's ways.

The first chapter, "The Christian in the World," rejects the notion that Christians should disengage from the world by separating themselves into enclaves or living "aloof from" the world. Rather, he upholds the idea that while "the Christian is necessarily *in* the world, he is not *of* it. This means that his thought, his life, and his heart are not controlled by the world and do not depend upon the world, for they belong to another Master."[60] Moreover, the Christian has been "sent into this world by this Master" because "he has a part to play in this world which no one else can possibly fulfill."[61] This part involves a "specific function" to be the salt of the earth, the light of the world, and a sheep among wolves. The first two images are drawn from Jesus' teaching in the Sermon on the Mount in Matt 5:13–16; the reference to sheep among wolves comes from Jesus' instructions to his disciples in Matt 10:16. The main emphasis is that the Christian is to be a "sign" of the reality of God's action in the world, someone who "reveals to the world the truth about its condition, and witnesses to the salvation of which he is an instrument."[62] Ellul focuses upon the strategic role of laypeople as Christ's representatives, those who are "involved in the life of the world through [their] work and his interests" because they face the acute pressures of the world's ways and values. It is critical to note that Ellul's theological understanding of the "world" is quite negative. The world is fallen, sinful, and hostile to Christians and the gospel, since it is "the domain of the Prince of this world, of Satan."[63] Because the gospel message itself is scandalous to the world, a faithful Christian should expect to be persecuted.

Ellul criticizes any attempts to diminish or escape the strong tension between Christian faith and life in the world and understands the layman as "the channel through which the gospel should reach the world" since he is "the point of contact between the ideologies of the world in which he lives and theology—between economic realities, and the forgiveness of Jesus Christ for those realities."[64] This must involve what Ellul calls an "agonistic" way of life, a life of constant struggle.[65] Faithfulness requires reliance

60. Ellul, *Presence*, 2.
61. Ibid., 2–3.
62. Ibid., 4.
63. Ibid., 9.
64. Ibid., 11.
65. Ibid., 13.

upon the Holy Spirit and prayer, as the Christian seeks to understand the realities of the world "on the spiritual plane" so that he or she can participate fully and effectively in the "preservation of the world" and its social or political life, "by the grace of God."[66]

The second chapter, "Revolutionary Christianity," takes up the discussion of "profound change, for a radical transformation of our present civilization" that was the subject of intense debate in the years immediately after World War II. At this point, Ellul begins to offer his analysis of "the constitutive elements of the modern world" as "the primacy of production, the continual growth of the power of the State and the formation of the National State, the autonomous development of technics, etc."[67] The most important feature is what he calls the "framework" or "essential structure" of modernity, which is to say, the belief that "increasing technical skill will bring men the greatest possible good. Yet all the catastrophes which afflict our epoch are connected with this framework."[68] A key concern for Ellul is the tendency to "subordinate man to his economic function," which leads to the "submergence of the 'person' in a mass-civilization."[69] This concern for the dehumanization of life is a pervasive theme of *The Presence of the Kingdom*.

In the face of this dehumanization, the world needs a "revolution" that brings about a new way of life: freedom from the tyranny of these "facts" and this reductionist framework. Ellul says, "If this revolution does not take place, we are done for, and human civilization as a whole is impossible."[70] Contending that Christianity has a "revolutionary character," Ellul argues that Christians must be "an inexhaustible revolutionary force in the midst of the world."[71] He explains that the Christian "belongs to two Cities" and lives in light of the certainty of the return of Jesus Christ to fulfill God's purposes—he is in the world, but "cannot wholly belong to this world."[72] Christians live in the midst of tension and opposition since they have "another Master" and also are citizens of God's kingdom, representing "another order" and "another claim."[73] Someone who is living by the power of Christ

---

66. Ellul, *Presence*, 19–20.
67. Ibid., 24.
68. Ibid.
69. Ibid., 25.
70. Ibid., 31.
71. Ibid.
72. Ibid., 33.
73. Ibid., 35.

is "a true revolutionary" who "makes the coming of the Kingdom actual" in everyday life.[74] How? Not naively pretending to "bring in" the kingdom or establishing a paradise, but working to make the world "tolerable," reducing the opposition between the disorder of the world and God's will for it, and supremely by proclaiming the good news of salvation.[75] This is what Ellul calls a Christian "style of life," which is a distinctive way of being in the world on behalf of Christ as salt, light, and a sheep among wolves.

The third chapter of *The Presence of the Kingdom*, "The End and the Means," expands on his critique of modern civilization, especially what he calls "technics"—which he would later describe more elaborately as "technique" in a series of major books. He states: "The first great fact that emerges from our civilization is that today everything has become 'means.' There is no longer an 'end'; we do not know whither we are going."[76] His examples are drawn from science and technology, where the values of efficiency and usefulness become dominant. An example is the idea found in the Nazi regime that "anyone who is not useful to the community must be put to death."[77] Along these lines, he adds: "no one knows where we are going, the aim of life has been forgotten, the end has been left behind. Man has set out at tremendous speed—to go *nowhere*."[78] The quest for "greater, quicker, more precise" takes over; "success" and "progress" are defined in purely technical ways and extended to all spheres of life. Society is increasingly in the hands of technicians who seek efficient results. These conditions make it "impossible to live one's faith."[79] In response, Ellul argues that "for Christians there is no dissociation between the end and the means" because in God's work, "the end and the means are the same."[80] In theological terms, the end (the kingdom of God), which will be established at the end of time, is "already present when the divine means (the only, unique, Mediator) is present."[81] He argues that the idea that means are spiritually and morally neutral is wrong. Instead, "all technical achievements are useless, unless they are controlled, given their right position, and judged by the coming

---

74. Ellul, *Presence*, 39.
75. Ibid., 35.
76. Ibid., 51.
77. Ibid., 53.
78. Ibid., 56. Italics in original.
79. Ibid., 77.
80. Ibid., 64.
81. Ibid., 65.

Kingdom of God."[82] Ellul returns to the theme of revolution, arguing that "unless the world can rediscover, by a spiritual revolution, an end whose presence can be perceived even in the secret world of technics, it is lost. Now we may search through all philosophies, but Christianity alone offers a solution."[83] The means of this spiritual revolution is simply that Christians would *live*, because "life, understood from the point of view of faith, has an extraordinary explosive force."[84]

Chapter 4, "The Problem of Communication," deals with the absence of genuine communication and human understanding in the modern world, a theme he would develop in later writings on propaganda. Ellul sees modern society as stubbornly unwilling to reckon with the reality of its condition. He detects a "refusal, unconscious but widespread, to become aware of reality. Man does not want to see himself in the real situation which the world constitutes for him. He refuses to see what it is that really constitutes our world."[85] He deals with the reductionist results that stem from embracing the notion that "all spheres of intelligence are, in fact, exploited by the technicians." What others have called "instrumental rationality" supplants contemplation.[86] In response, he calls Christians to particular tasks. "The first duty of a Christian intellectual today is the duty of awareness: that is to say, the duty of understanding the world and oneself, inseparably connected and inseparably condemned, in their reality."[87] He calls Christians to intentionally restore personal contact with their neighbors, and to think of a specific person rather than an abstracted humanity. But his main point is a summons to action: "What we need is to find the true structure or framework of our modern civilization, though in order to get down to this we may have to do a great deal of difficult and delicate scraping away of extraneous matter. We need to understand this framework as the expression of the spiritual reality of our civilization."[88] This awareness implies an "engagement (or act of resolute committal)," which is not merely the work of an observer or spectator, but the work of a sign or symbol pointing toward Christ by giving "more direction to the world in the spheres of

---

82. Ellul, *Presence*, 71.
83. Ibid., 73.
84. Ibid., 77.
85. Ibid., 82.
86. Ibid., 92.
87. Ibid., 98.
88. Ibid., 100.

politics, social conditions, and many others" so that modern culture might "find *a hope which is no illusion*."[89] He concludes: "The work of Christian intellectuals is not done in the abstract: it is effective participation in the preservation of the world, and in the building up of the church."[90]

This synopsis shows that *The Presence of the Kingdom* anticipates and introduces most of the key themes that preoccupied Ellul throughout his many writings: the need for distinctively Christian engagement in the world; the analysis of the social and spiritual conditions of modern civilization; the nature of transformation or "revolution"; the inexorable dynamics of means, as well as the triumph of "technics" (or technique) with their drive toward efficiency in all sectors of life and their attendant threat of dehumanization; the breakdown of human communication and the eclipse of the genuine search for truth as a result of the ascendency of technical rationality; and the incomparable and irreplaceable revelation of Jesus Christ as the only source of hope. As we consider Ellul's thinking on technology, propaganda, the city, political economy, Scripture, and ethics, and as we consider his approach to integrating faith, life, and scholarship, we will see that these themes and threads play an organizing role. These, along with a consistent commitment to the command of Rom 12:2—"do not conform to the pattern of this world, but be transformed by the renewing of your mind"—shed much light on Ellul's work, as we will see in the coming chapters.

---

89. Ibid., 100, 109. Italics added.
90. Ibid., 112.

CHAPTER 2

Technology and Technique

"Efficiency is a fact and justice a slogan."[1]

ELLUL IS BEST KNOWN for his writings on technology and technique. Indeed, some regard Ellul chiefly as a critic of technology. Two days after his death on May 19, 1994, Ellul's obituary in *The New York Times* read, "Jacques Ellul, French Critic of Technology, Is Dead at 82." While some assessments of Ellul's work unfairly characterize him either as a Luddite crank or as a scholar narrowly focused on technology, it is true that technology and technique are a major theme of his work. His best-selling book was *The Technological Society*, which earned him notoriety on both sides of the Atlantic and placed him among the ranks of important European and American voices—including Martin Heidegger and Lewis Mumford—interrogating the role of technology in twentieth-century life.

When it was first published in France in the fall of 1954, *The Technological Society* was titled, *La Technique ou l'enjeu du siècle*. A direct translation would be *Technique, or the Stake of the Century*, where the word *stake* translates the French *enjeu*, which is a contraction of *en jeu* or *in play*, meaning what is at stake in a game and referring to the money that one puts *in play* at the beginning of a game and that returns to the winner. What, exactly, was at stake? And what was the game? According to Ellul, nothing less than the future of humanity was at stake in our relationship to the methods and machines of industry and convenience. "The Society of

---

1. Ellul, *Technological Society*, 282.

Efficient Techniques"—a better translation of the book's title, according to Darrell Fasching—favored artifice over nature and necessity over freedom. Technical capabilities and commitments that were supposed to free us from the vicissitudes of nature had, in fact, enslaved us and created a new and equally threatening environment:[2]

> Technique has penetrated the deepest recesses of the human being. The machine tends not only to create a new human environment, but also to modify man's very essence. The milieu in which he lives is no longer his. He must adapt himself, as though the world were new, to a universe for which he was not created. He was made to go six kilometers an hour, and he goes a thousand. He was made to eat when he was hungry and to sleep when he was sleepy; instead, he obeys a clock. He was made to have contact with living things, and he lives in a world of stone. He was created with a certain essential unity, and he is fragmented by all the forces of the modern world.[3]

The origins and implications of this situation were the topic of Ellul's best-known book and a persistent theme throughout his *corpus*. Ellul's statement pronounces clearly his desperate cry of the heart. He is profoundly concerned for the dehumanizing impact of a world driven by an alien, technological mindset. According to Ellul, something deeply or even essentially human is being lost as human beings increasingly conform to an artificial environment oriented by machines and their logic. In this book we want to argue that just beneath the surface of Ellul's statement is a deeply Christian view of the nature of human flourishing. Even though Ellul's social and cultural analysis of technology does not often make overt references to his Christian faith, nevertheless his faith-informed perspective on what makes human life meaningful can be recognized throughout.

The Technological Society: Historical Context and Reception

The Technological Society was published in a decade of considerable social and technological change: *Playboy* magazine was launched in December 1953, the McDonald's restaurant chain was opened in April 1955, followed by the opening of a California theme park called Disneyland in July 1955. Television was becoming a mass medium by which these brands would

2. Fasching, *Thought of Jacques Ellul*, 15.
3. Ellul, *Technological Society*, 325.

eventually capture the imagination of billions of households around the world. All of these developments took place in the shadow of great foreboding, as the Cold War and attendant arms race threatened nuclear annihilation, a novel possibility. It was in this context that Ellul made the audacious claim, "No social, human, or spiritual fact is so important as the fact of technique in the modern world."[4] In other words, according to Ellul the student of social institutions, technique and technology actually were the controlling social institutions of his time.

At 449 pages, and with another ten years before it would see translation and publication into English, the book was met with a mixture of intrigue and serious reservations. Sociologist Rupert Vance noted that, while the book was worth reading and "could not be ruled off course," Ellul ascribed to technologies, or means, the moral dereliction that can only be assigned to our ends or goals and that "like most purveyors of doom, Ellul rides his ideas too hard."[5] Futurist Alvin Toffler noted that while Ellul's books, especially *The Technological Society*, enjoyed "a campus vogue," Ellul himself was one of the most extreme of "a generation of future haters and technophobes."[6] Howard Falk was more ambivalent in his assessment. He claimed that Ellul's analysis was both self-contradictory and one-sided, ignoring the vast range of forces shaping modern life; yet, Falk wrote, Ellul's approach was a "valuable means of reexamining questions which have become almost too familiar."[7] Perhaps the reviewer who liked the book best was the Trappist monk Thomas Merton, who had already chosen a life of resistance to modernity and a deep commitment to the practice of the Christian faith. Merton said it was "one of the most important books of this mid-century."[8] These comments reflect the persistent controversy surrounding Ellul's provocative ideas concerning technology.

Technique and Technological Society

For Ellul, technique and technology were the most important facts of the twentieth century; focusing on them would bring to light the most important questions for any theorist undertaking an analysis of social realities.

---

4. Ibid., 3.
5. Vance, review of *Technological Society*, 417.
6. Toffler, *Future Shock*, 319.
7. Falk, review of *Technological Society*, 532.
8. Merton, review of *Technological Society*, 385.

Understanding Jacques Ellul

As Ellul wrote, technology and technique deserved a central place in mid-twentieth-century social thought, a place analogous to that which Marx gave to capital.

> I was strongly influenced by Marx when I was young and the question for me was "if Marx was writing now . . . would he bring all his analysis to bear on the problem of capital and its accumulation? Would there not be another more important question in his eyes?" Together with one or two friends, we thought that the central question was the development of *la technique* and that it was necessary to undertake an analysis of the technical phenomenon as Marx had attempted to analyze capital.[9]

By "technological society," Ellul referred to a civilization in which technique had become an organizing force parallel to Marx's idea of capital. But what, for Ellul, was technique?

Types of Technique

By the French phrase "*la technique*," Ellul did not simply mean "technology" or "technologies." Rather, he meant "the totality of methods rationally arrived at and having absolute efficiency (for a given stage of development) in every field of human activity."[10] The role of technique is to clarify, arrange, rationalize, and "bring efficiency to everything."[11] Technique includes machinery and other technologies, as well as methods for organizing human activity in ways that maximize the ratio of output to input. Importantly, however, for Ellul technique is greater than the sum of individual parts or means. While "technique is nothing more than means and the ensemble of means,"[12] it is simultaneously "much more complex than any synthesis of characteristics common to individual techniques . . . it is the method which characterizes the operation [of all individual techniques]."[13]

Ellul saw three principal subdivisions of technique: economic, organizational, and human. *Economic techniques* are aimed at production of goods and include everything from the organization of production in a

---

9. "Jacques Ellul, theologien de l'esperance." *Le Quotidien de Paris* (January 27, 1981). Translated by and cited in Goddard, *Living the Word*, 22.
10. Ellul, *Technological Society*, xxv.
11. Ibid., 5.
12. Ibid., 19.
13. Ibid.

given factory or corporation—the assembly line, for example—to national economic planning. *Organizational technique* is applied to administration, law, police power, and warfare. *Human technique* is aimed at accommodating humans to other techniques through propaganda, medicine, genetic engineering, and other means. When, for example, the drudgery and alienation of factory employment under the conditions of economic technique induces depression and a feeling of disconnection from nature and human community, there are human techniques—pharmacology, for example—that can be applied to ameliorate the situation.

The Preconditions of Technological Society

Ellul situates his account of technique in a sweeping historical narrative. The technological society was that which followed the industrial society, and it was a society for which techniques and technologies had become the driving forces, the dominant milieu or environment in which human beings found themselves. He theorizes that before that transition could happen, however, certain preconditions had to be met. These included a long technical incubation in which specific techniques were permitted to proliferate in relatively unchecked fashion. The human population had to grow so large that only the most efficient means of provision could satisfy its needs. The economic system had to be stable enough to prevent great upheaval while being dynamic enough to provide a platform for technical change. Society had to become more flexible: social groups, such as castes, and other social institutions, like the church, had largely to be marginalized or eliminated so that social change became possible for the individual and so that competition to guide individual commitments and ambitions would be decreased. Ellul writes that all of these are combined through "a clear technical intention,"[14] which combines the effects of the other four preconditions and directs them toward efficiency.[15] Under these conditions, technique can become the all-embracing consciousness of the mechanical world.

14. Ibid., 52.
15. Ibid., 45–60.

Understanding Jacques Ellul

The Seven Characteristics of Technique

In the second chapter of *Technological Society*, Ellul offers a "characterology of technique," which he describes as "the psychology of the tyrant" who holds power over technological society.[16] In it, he identifies seven characteristics of technique. The first two, rationality and artificiality, are the basis for five more that will require more detailed explanation.

By rationality, Ellul means a commitment to "bring mechanics to bear on all that is spontaneous and irrational."[17] This, he indicates, is "best exemplified in systematization, division of labor, creation of standards, production norms and the like";[18] each of these involves two distinct phases: "the use of 'discourse' in every operation that excludes spontaneity and personal creativity,"[19] and the reduction of "facts, forces, phenomena, means and instruments to the schema of logic."[20] By artificiality, Ellul means that "technique is opposed to nature" in so much as it "destroys, eliminates, or subordinates the natural world, and does not allow this world to restore itself or even to enter into a symbiotic relation with it."[21] Rationality introduces the prospect that there is but one best solution to any given problem, and the rationalizing impulse takes this approach to all problems. Artifice militates against nature and leans toward the creation of a novel environment or milieu for human development. Both of these impulses are directed toward overcoming necessity and freeing human beings from the tyranny of scarcity, tragedy, and risk. Coupled with automatism, self-augmentation, monism, universalism, and autonomy, though, these impulses actually subvert the purposes toward which they were originally directed and ultimately cause human submission to a new technical form of necessity.

1. Automatism of technical choice—Automatism is the first characteristic of technique. By automatism Ellul meant that technique "automatically" decides for itself, independently of human judgments, what the "one best

---

16. Ellul, *Technological Society*, 147.
17. Ibid., 78–79.
18. Ibid., 79.
19. Ibid.
20. Ibid.
21. Ibid.

way" for achieving a result is:

> When everything has been measured and calculated mathematically so that the method which has been decided upon is satisfactory from the rational point of view, and when, from the practical point of view, the method is manifestly the most efficient of all those hitherto employed or those in competition with it, then the technical movement becomes self-directing. I call this process automatism.
>
> There is no personal choice, in respect to magnitude, between, say, 3 and 4; 4 is greater than 3; this is a fact which has no personal reference. No one can change it or assert the contrary or personally escape it . . . Technique itself, *ipso facto* and without indulgence or possible human discussion, selects among the means to be employed. . . . If a machine can yield a given result, it must be used to capacity, and it is considered criminal and antisocial not to do so.[22]

Notice here that the erosion of reasoned human judgment and choice is central to Ellul's concern and that the result is a loss of a basic human freedom by the imposition of a new social convention. Ellul characterizes automatism with the straightforward phrase "the one best way."[23] Technique identifies and valorizes the single most efficient way to do anything. As such, it is inherently reductionist.

The "one best way" is taken from an American, Frederick Winslow Taylor (1856–1915), the father of scientific management, who coined the term to describe the outcome of his time studies that were integral to improving industrial efficiency.[24] It can be argued that this approach was later extended to rule virtually all forms of human activity: "It ranges from the act of shaving to the act of organizing the landing at Normandy . . . today no human activity escapes this technical imperative. There is a technique of organization . . . just as there is a technique of friendship and a technique of swimming."[25] The "one best way" is thus the way that is the most efficient, which is the way that uses the least time, motion, energy, or investment. You need not look far in today's world to see that *the one best way* rules everything, from the one best posture for sitting at your computer to the one best method for avoiding carpal tunnel syndrome. As David Wang writes, "Such a cultural consciousness focuses exclusively on evolving new

22. Ellul, *Technological Society*, 80–81.
23. See ibid., 70, 97, 130.
24. Taylor, *Principles of Scientific Management*.
25. Ellul, *Technological Society*, 21–22.

methods, from making friends to making war. In this respect, for example, the dating service eHarmony.com shares common ground with organizing the Iraq Surge; all we need are the right techniques."[26]

The automatism of technique and its seeking the one best way militate against human freedom:

> The individual is in a dilemma: either he decides to safeguard his freedom of choice, chooses to use traditional, personal, moral, or empirical means, thereby entering into competition with a power against which there is no efficacious defense and before which he must suffer defeat; or he decides to accept technical necessity, in which case he will himself be the victor, but only by submitting irreparably to technical slavery. In effect he has no freedom of choice.[27]

This statement reveals a key theme in Ellul's considerations about the full range of social and cultural matters: the tension between freedom and necessity. The ability of human beings to make deliberate choices about their behavior, even with regard to small matters of daily life, is jeopardized by the dominance of what he calls "technical necessity," the powerful drive to conform to what an impersonal technological system has impersonally determined as the best way to operate. For Ellul, as human beings more fully allow themselves to be directed and oriented by such impersonal pressures and conditions, the less human they become.

2. *Self-augmentation*—The second characteristic of technique is "self-augmentation," which refers to the capacity of technique to engender further commitments to and developments in technique. Ellul points out that "the number of scientists and technicians has doubled every decade for a century and a half. Apparently this is a self-generating process: technique engenders itself."[28] Specifically, Ellul argues that "self-augmentation can be formulated to two laws: 1. In a given civilization, technical progress is irreversible. 2. Technical progress tends to act, not according to an arithmetic, but according to a geometric progression."[29]

Of the first law Ellul says that nontechnical conditions are not determinative in technical developments. "We can no longer argue that it is an economic or a social condition, or education, or any other human factor"

---

26. Wang, "Ellul on New Urbanism," 461–62.
27. Ellul, *Technological Society*, 84.
28. Ibid., 87.
29. Ibid., 89.

that determines technological progress. On the contrary, technical developments themselves determine consequent technical developments: "Essentially, the preceding technical situation alone is determinative. When a given technical discovery occurs, it has followed almost of necessity certain other discoveries."[30] Of the second law, technical progress evolves according to a geometric progression because "a technical discovery has repercussions and entails progress in several branches of technique and not merely one. Moreover, techniques combine with one another, and the more given techniques there are to be combined, the more combinations are possible."[31]

3. *Monism*—Monism, by which Ellul meant indivisibility, is the third characteristic of technique. According to Ellul, technique "forms a whole" and "presents, everywhere and essentially, the same characteristics."[32] In other words, the characteristics and effects of technologies are not dependent upon the uses to which they are put; technologies are not neutral, and their ill effects must be taken with the good—they are indivisible:

> The great tendency of all persons who study techniques is to make distinctions. They distinguish between the different elements of technique, maintaining some and discarding others. They distinguish between technique and the use to which it is put. These distinctions are completely invalid and show only that he who makes them has understood nothing of the technical phenomenon. Its parts are ontologically tied together; in it, use is inseparable from being.[33]

So technique cannot be turned for good or for ill by humans who presume to direct it. For example, nuclear energy is a technology to which the argument for neutrality has often been applied. The common refrain is that nuclear energy can be used either to *power cities* or *destroy cities*—that each user determines the end to which nuclear technology is put. Ellul suggests otherwise:

> If atomic research is encouraged, it is obligatory to pass through the stage of the atomic bomb; the bomb represents by far the

30. Ellul, *Technological Society*, 90.
31. Ibid., 91.
32. Ibid., 94.
33. Ibid., 95. Marshall McLuhan makes essentially the same point when he writes, "Our conventional response to all media, namely that it is how they are used that counts, is the numb stance of the technological idiot" (*Understanding Media*, 11, 18).

simplest utilization of atomic energy. The problems involved in the military use of atomic energy are infinitely more simple to resolve than are those involved in its industrial use. . . . The experience of Great Britain between 1955 and 1960[34] in producing electricity of nuclear origin is very significant in this respect.[35]

Even once peaceful intentions for nuclear power were realized, they were accompanied by what Ellul would have regarded as inevitable downsides—accidents at Three Mile Island, Chernobyl, and Fukushima, as well as failures to safely and securely store nuclear material. In other words, according to Ellul, we must accept the good and bad effects of nuclear technology together, and this "indivisibility" applies to other techniques, as well. Put another way, Ellul would agree with the statement that you cannot have the benefits of a five-thousand-channel universe without a little attention deficit disorder to go with it.

4. *Technical universalism*—According to Ellul, prior to the eighteenth century, technique was sporadic, local, and culturally restrained by custom, tradition, myth, and belief. Ellul believed that what he described in 1954 was radically different from all that had come before in human history. Technique comes along with universal ambitions. If realized, the one best way in Uganda would be no different from the one best way in the United States. Ellul claimed that "from the geographic point of view, it is easy to see that technique is constantly gaining ground, country by country, and that its area of action is the whole world."[36] While "in the course of history there have always been different principles of civilization according to regions, nations, and continents . . . today everything tends to align itself on technical principles."[37] Technical universalism leads, according to Ellul, toward homogeneity until "[t]echnique is the same in all latitudes and hence acts to make different civilizations uniform."[38] In this way, technique

---

34. The English translation of *The Technological Society* was updated by Ellul in June 1963 prior to publication, which is why this post-1954 datum, among others, is in the American edition.
35. Ellul, *Technological Society*, 99.
36. Ibid., 116.
37. Ibid., 117.
38. Ibid.

strikes at the heart of diversity and at the integrity of the individual.

5. *The autonomy of technique*—By autonomy Ellul meant technique must and will always end up working independently of other considerations. Just as Frederick Winslow Taylor viewed the industrial plant as a "whole in itself, a 'closed organism,' an end in itself," so too must technique be "autonomous with respect to economics and politics."[39] In Ellul's assessment, "Autonomy is the essential condition for the development of technique," which then goes on to become the primary driver of everything else. And here is where Ellul comes in for charges of being a reductionistic "technological determinist," claiming that nothing conditions technique and that technique conditions everything else.

> Technique elicits and conditions social, political, and economic change. It is the prime mover of all the rest, in spite of any appearance to the contrary and in spite of human pride, which pretends that man's philosophical theories are still determining influences and man's political regimes decisive factors in technical evolution. External necessities no longer determine technique. Technique's own internal necessities are determinative. Technique has become a reality in itself, self-sufficient, with its special laws and determinations.[40]

Ellul was especially attuned to what he saw as a problematic relationship between technical reasoning and moral and spiritual reasoning. Rather than moral and spiritual reasoning determining our relationship to and use of technology and technique, technical reasoning determines what is moral and what is the value of the spiritual. Ellul writes, "To go one step further, technical autonomy is apparent in respect to morality and spiritual values. Technique tolerates no judgment from without and accepts no limitations . . . Since it has put itself beyond good and evil, it need fear no limitation whatever."[41] In technological society, efficiency, rather than goodness, truth, beauty, or justice, becomes the norming norm for social relations.

---

39. Ibid., 133.
40. Ibid., 133–34.
41. Ibid., 134.

The Biggest Conspiracy Is This: There Is No Conspiracy

While technique creates an elite group whose function is simply to execute techniques and who may be perceived as conspiracists, according to Ellul, this is not so. The impersonality of technique means that there is neither a cabal nor a conspiracy controlling or dictating developments in technological society. As Robert Merton says succinctly in his foreword to the book, "Only the naïve can really believe that the world-wide movement toward centralism results from the machinations of evil statesmen."[42] As Ellul writes,

> It is not the result of a plot or plan by any one man or any group of men who direct it or apply it or shunt it in new directions. The technical phenomenon is impersonal and in following its course we have found that it is directed toward man. . . . Proceeding at its own tempo, technique analyzes its objects so that it can reconstitute them; in the case of man, it has analyzed him and synthesized a hitherto unknown being.[43]

If one follows Ellul's logic, then the good news is that there is no conspiracy; on the other hand, the bad news is that there is no conspiracy. Impersonal technique creates a totalizing system of organized, collective irresponsibility—that is, no one person or group of people is empowered to exercise the freedom of choice required for responsible action, nor can one person or group be held accountable for developments in technological society.

The Spiritual Consequences of Technique

According to Ellul, the ascendance of technological society has spiritual, as well as social, consequences. In its autonomy, technique gives its own law, becoming the transcendent norm by which we judge not only between right and wrong but also between competing rights. And this autonomy "renders technique at once sacrilegious and sacred:"[44]

> The invasion of technique desacralizes the world in which man is called upon to live. For technique nothing is sacred, there is

---

42. Merton, foreword to *Technological Society*, vii.
43. Ellul, *Technological Society*, 387–88.
44. Ibid., 141.

> no mystery, no taboo. . . . Technique worships nothing, respects nothing. . . . Science brings to the light of day everything man had believed sacred. Technique takes possession of it and enslaves it. . . . Technique denies mystery a priori. The mysterious is merely that which has not yet been technicized. . . . Nothing belongs any longer to the realm of gods or the supernatural. The individual who lives in the technical milieu knows very well that there is nothing spiritual anywhere. . . . He therefore transfers his sense of the sacred to the very thing which has destroyed its former object: to technique itself.[45]

For Ellul, this conjures the principalities and powers of Ephesians 6:12: "For our struggle is not against flesh and blood, but against the rulers, against the authorities, against the powers of this dark world and against the spiritual forces of evil in the heavenly realms." Thus, it should not come as a surprise that for Ellul there were three realms in which the powers of this dark world and the spiritual forces of evil did their primary work: technique, commerce, and the state.[46] It is again important not to misunderstand what Ellul meant in this regard: he did not state or imply that technology (or any specific technology) was inherently evil, that capitalism (or socialism, or any specific economic system) was inherently evil, or that democracy (or monarchy, or any specific political state) was inherently evil. Rather, he argued that the realms of technique, commerce, and the state were the three realms where the principalities and powers seemed to have the most success in limiting human freedoms, imposing their own tyrannies, and doing so precisely because of features or characteristics endemic to their structure, process, or function, each operating according to the necessities imposed by the dominance of technique.

The seven characteristics of technique may sound like long, complex, and somewhat discrete theories Ellul offers about our age. But if you look at one particular technique, and see how it works, Ellul's seven characteristics show themselves to be remarkably interconnected. Consider the technique of the automobile, the twentieth century's "one best way" to approach transportation challenges.

1. The *rationality* of the automobile is evidenced in the industry's history from almost the earliest days to now. Henry Ford's assembly line is perhaps one of the earliest examples of a true "systemization, division

---

45. Ibid., 142–43. This was precisely Neil Postman's point in *Technopoly*, a work greatly influenced by Ellul.

46. See, among others, Ellul, *Ellul on Religion, Technology, and Politics*, 113–14.

of labor, creation of standards, production norms and the like." That this system for producing automobiles "excludes spontaneity and personal creativity" and reduces "facts, forces, phenomena, means and instruments to the schema of logic" is testified by all car factories everywhere. Though we now take it for granted, the emergence of Taylorist/Fordist production practices was such a significant, large, and observable phenomenon in the 1930s that Aldous Huxley divided time itself into "Before Ford (BF)" and "After Ford (AF)" in his dystopian novel of the future, *Brave New World*.

2. The *artificiality* of the technique of the automobile is evident in many ways, from how the car destroys the countryside to how the highway system is itself the largest manmade object in existence (when viewed as one "thing"), taking up a global area of roughly eleven million miles of pavement. Marshall McLuhan said that the car turns the driver into a "misguided missile," and James Howard Kunstler, in his book *The Geography of Nowhere*, does an excellent job of detailing the ways in which the car created suburbia and destroyed the human scale of American cities and towns.

3. The *automatism* of the car is, of course, self-evident inasmuch as the *automobile* and *automatism* share the same metaphoric root. The car is auto-mobile: it moves itself. The automobile is indifferent to human judgments about what the one best way is. Thus the width of the lane of a road, the straightness of a highway needed to maintain minimum traveling speeds, and similar considerations all make many human factors irrelevant, a fact most poignantly illustrated by the destruction of multiple neighborhoods when city planner Robert Moses remade New York for the automobile from the 1930s to the 1960s.

4. The *self-augmentation* of the automobile is evident in many ways. New versions of existing car models are produced every year, and brand-new models introduced within a brand every few years. The automobile is the primary mode of transportation in most developed countries, accounting for more than eight hundred million vehicles on the world's roads at present. In the United States, the number of licensed vehicles has long surpassed the number of licensed drivers. From a consumer behavior point of view, many critics have pointed out how the automobile has become a fashion statement or accessory and has gone from being a durable good that can last for twenty to

forty years to being a disposable good whose symbolic life is only three to five years, after which point it needs replacing in order for the owner to feel "current." Thus, one of the ways that the automobile self-augments has been to convert itself from a mode of conveyance to a status symbol that its user "wears."

5. The *monism* of the automobile is evident in the indivisibility of its good from its bad effects. You cannot create a vehicle designed to take its passengers ten times their normal walking speed and not accept the fatalities that ensue. Likewise, the internal combustion engine, for all of its benefits, introduces certain costs, including human and ecological devastation attendant to the extraction of oil and combustion of gasoline. At best, the only thing possible are trade-offs, such as the trade-off between the American highway system and the German autobahn—in America there are speed limits and a high number of traffic accidents every year, many of which are fatal; in Germany's autobahn system there is no speed limit and there is, counterintuitively, a lower number of accidents, though a higher percentage of accidents are fatal.

6. The *universalism* of the automobile is the sameness that it tends to create across geographical borders. This production of homogenous effects across cultures may help explain why Venice, Italy, is such a highly vaunted tourist destination: it is one of the few places in the industrialized world where you can get away from the car and the culture it both assumes and creates. You also see the effect in reverse in those places that do not accept the totality of these homogenizing effects. The use of horse and buggies in many Amish communities is seen as the exception that both proves and defines the norm: they are seen as unusual (and their communities have become tourist destinations) largely because they do not drive cars.

7. The *autonomy* of the automobile is "apparent in respect to morality and spiritual values."[47] The automobile "tolerates no judgment from without and accepts no limitations. . . . Since it has put itself beyond good and evil, it need fear no limitation whatever."[48] Rather than judge the technology according to moral and spiritual values, the car stands alone as an independent feature of modern life, one taken for granted

47. Ellul, *Technological Society*, 134.
48. Ibid.

rather than interrogated from an ethical point of view. The annual human death toll caused by the automobile is nothing less than astonishing, both locally and globally. Traffic collisions have killed between thirty and ninety million people since the advent of the automobile. Every six hours, such accidents kill eight hundred people and injure more than thirty-four thousand.[49] If we imagine any new technology being introduced with this death toll as one of the "side effects," we would think twice about its merits. However, we find ourselves curiously unable to judge the automobile as a technology or vehicular deaths according to ethical standards. The cause of a vehicle-related accident is almost always the driver, the alcohol, the weather, the road conditions, a fault in the automobile's design, or some combination thereof; it is never attributed to the car itself. Currently, there are about thirty-three thousand traffic-related deaths in America each year, and about 1.2 million worldwide. Globally, car crashes are the number one killer of young people. In 1947 one of these fatalities was Simon, Jacques and Yvette Ellul's six-year-old son, who died after being hit by a car while crossing the street. *The Meaning of the City*, which will be examined in chapter 4, is dedicated to his memory.

Ellul's Hope

Ellul's hope in the face of these developments was twofold. First, he believed strongly in human free will, the capacity to direct one's way of life and take decisive action. As we will show in later chapters, he has a positive view of humanity's capacity for resisting the pressures of technique, a task that is difficult but not impossible, in his judgment. In the 1963 revision of *The Technological Society*, he writes:

> There will be a temptation to use the word *fatalism* in connection with the phenomena described in this book. The reader may be inclined to say that, if everything happens as stated in the book, man is entirely helpless—helpless either to preserve his personal freedom or to change the course of events. Once again, I think the

---

49. Peter Dauvergne points out that this time frame—six hours—was the time required for the jury to deliver a verdict in the first case of an automobile death. The jury found the driver innocent, and the coroner expressed his hope that such a tragedy would never happen again. For the fascinating and tragic story of the first automobile death and the legal case surrounding the incident, see Dauvergne, "Accidental Dependency."

question is badly put. I would reverse the terms and say: if man—if each one of us—abdicates his responsibilities with regard to values; if each of us limits himself to leading a trivial existence in a technological civilization, with greater adaptation and increasing success as his sole objectives; if we do not even consider the possibility of making a stand against these determinants, then everything will happen as I have described it, and the determinants will be transformed into inevitabilities.[50]

Ellul concludes the foreword to the revised American edition of *The Technological Society* with a restatement of this dynamic that emphasizes freedom in the face of necessity:

As a matter of fact, reality is itself a combination of determinisms, and freedom consists in overcoming and transcending these determinisms. Freedom is completely without meaning unless it is related to necessity, unless it represents victory over necessity. . . . We must not think of the problem in terms of a choice between being determined and being free. We must look at it dialectically, and say that man is indeed determined, but that it is open to him to overcome necessity, and that this *act* is freedom. Freedom is not static but dynamic; not a vested interest, but a prize continually to be won. The moment man stops and resigns himself, he becomes subject to determinism. He is most enslaved when he thinks he is comfortably settled in freedom.[51]

This dialectical understanding means that human beings must always be vigilant and alert lest they become dehumanized and enslaved by blind, naïve adherence to the patterns imposed, silently (and often invisibly) yet powerfully, by technique. In advocating this stance of resistance and vigilance, Ellul's Christian faith was a major source of his hope in human freedom despite the apparent dominance of technique. For Ellul, the revelation of God in Christ was ultimately a message of liberation against which no enslaving system could stand. Christianity was an "anti-religious" faith. For Ellul, as for Barth, the distinction between faith and religion was significant: *religion* was a human invention created to constrain human freedom, and this was radically opposed by the Christ of whom Paul said, "It is for freedom that Christ has set us free. Stand firm, then, and do not let yourselves be burdened again by a yoke of slavery" (Gal 5:1).

---

50. Ellul, *Technological Society.*, xxix.
51. Ibid., xxxii–xxxiii.

For Ellul, freedom in the end is assured because of the work of Jesus Christ. In the meantime, Christians are called to exercise what freedom they have by profaning technology—deconstructing its soteriological myth—and refusing to submit to technological necessity. This does not mean opting out of all use of technology. Rather, it means consciously choosing—knowing both the upsides and downsides of any technique or machine—whether or not to use it, rather than simply saying that one *must* use it.

Conclusion

In the final chapters of *The Technological Society*, Ellul presents a vision so bleak that he said of it, "Here is a future Huxley [in *Brave New World*] never dreamed of."[52] Significantly, Ellul's future technological society might be seen as combining features of the dystopian futures envisioned by both Aldous Huxley (in *Brave New World*, 1932) and George Orwell (in *1984*, 1948). It is a totalitarian society in which rules are enforced by pleasure, à la Huxley, in which "we shall be rewarded with everything our hearts ever desired."[53] But it is also a world of totalitarianism in which "technique means not comfort, but power"[54] and in which man must be made, like Winston Smith, to love Big Brother, and this is its genius: "It makes men happy in a milieu which normally would have made them unhappy."[55] What Ellul saw was the totality of technique, its complete penetration of man's outer and inner worlds, its creation of entirely new necessities for human submission, its bondage of human freedom, and how this was the new, largest, most pressing and defining problem of the age. With this work he attempted to answer the call of one of his earliest essays: he had become the very thing he had claimed was needed just seven years earlier—a new Karl Marx. In that essay, Ellul said that "we must try to pose clearly the foundational problems"[56] and claimed that Marx was the metaphor of what was needed because "Marx was the only man of his time who grasped

52. Ibid., 433.
53. Ibid., 427.
54. Ibid., 421.
55. Ibid., 348. See Postman, *Amusing Ourselves to Death*, and Terlizzese, *Hope in the Thought of Jacques Ellul*, for a more thorough discussion on the question of whether our contemporary world is a fulfillment of the Huxleyan or Orwellian future.
56. Ellul, "New Karl Marx," 37.

the totality of the social, political, and economic problems in their reality and posed correctly the questions facing the civilization of the nineteenth century."[57] In *The Technological Society*, Ellul attempts to grasp the totality of the social, political, and economic problems in their reality and to pose correctly some of the most essential questions facing the global civilization of the late twentieth century.[58]

In later books, most notably *The Technological System* (1977 originally, 1980 in translation) and *The Technological Bluff* (1988 originally, 1990 in translation), Ellul further refined his thinking on technique's influence over all of civilization. These two works are worth reading, as they both enhance comprehension of *The Technological Society* and show Ellul refining his arguments as both his understanding and modern technologies evolve. In brief, the technological system for Ellul signifies the way in which a given technique is not simply "in and of itself" but is entirely interdependent with many other techniques, all of which require each other for continued sustenance. The technological bluff, on the other hand, is the "bluff" that technology, as a mode of discourse, makes in persuading its users that the benefits outweigh the costs and that technological "progress" is therefore worth it when, in fact, the opposite is true: "every technical application from its beginnings presents certain unforeseeable secondary effects which are much more disastrous than the lack of technique would have been."[59] In the French, the wordplay of his titles is deliberate and works to form a comprehensive whole: the bluff (*le bluff*) is what makes you fall for the game of technique and is what prevents you from seeing what is at stake (*l'enjeu*), which of course is everything. The game is upon us, and why we keep falling for it is a function of propaganda, one of the game's most refined techniques.

---

57. Ibid., 39.

58. Some readers may have encountered "76 Questions concerning Technology," which some have attributed to Ellul. While it is certainly plausible that the document was inspired by Ellul's work, it is not clear that Ellul was the author. In light of difficulties identifying the author of the document, it is important to note that claims that he wrote or compiled the questions may be apocryphal.

59. Ellul, *Technological Society*, 105.

CHAPTER 3

Communication: Media, Propaganda, and the Word

> *"For today's individual a fact is the ultimate reason, the supreme value, and an unimpeachable proof. Everything bows before a fact. We must obey it. We are irrational, idealistic dreamers if we do not trust facts. It is not enough to take facts into account; we also attribute decisive value to them. No justice, truth, or humanity can stand up in the face of a fact. It decides everything."*[1]

ACCORDING TO ELLUL, IN technological society, efficiency becomes the decisive aspect of human existence. Through the machinery and methods of convenience and industry, it comes to determine the shape of all other aspects of life, from transportation to medicine to friendship. According to two of Ellul's most important works, it is also a decisive influence upon communication. The effects of modern thought and life upon media and propaganda dehumanize communication and undermine notions of and access to truth.

Propaganda

In its original cultural, historical, and linguistic context, the term *propaganda* simply meant the means by which a message was "propagated" in the sense of being transmitted. Indeed, its earliest uses referred to the means by

---

1. Ellul, *Humiliation of the Word*, 137.

which the church would communicate the message of the gospel to unbelievers in order to promote orthodoxy. By the mid-twentieth century, any neutral or positive connotation of the term was gone. Propaganda had come to be understood as a technique for manipulating thoughts, emotions, and behaviors, a means of whipping up a crowd much like the one that Ellul observed at a Nazi rally during his 1935 visit to Munich. Indeed, Adolf Hitler himself had given considerable thought to the use of propaganda well before his rise to power. In 1914, authoring *Mein Kampf* from a prison cell, Hitler wrote that propaganda was the key to the "heart of the masses":

> The more modest [propaganda's] intellectual ballast, the more exclusively it takes into consideration the emotions of the masses, the more effective it will be. And this is the best proof of the soundness or unsoundness of a propaganda campaign, and not success in pleasing a few scholars or young aesthetes. The art of propaganda lies in understanding the emotional ideas of the great masses and finding, through a psychologically correct form, the way to the attention and thence to the heart of the broad masses.[2]

By the end of World War II, the word *propaganda* had come to evoke the notorious Reich Ministry of Public Enlightenment and Propaganda headed by Joseph Goebbels. Goebbels, who held a PhD in literature, had been taking his cues from Edward Bernays' 1923 book *Crystallizing Public Opinion*, a landmark text on the technique of public relations.

Within two decades of World War II, Ellul wrote his study of propaganda. Published in 1962, his book-length treatise on the subject followed after the sketches of human technique that he offered in *The Technological Society*. The English translation of *Propaganda* was published in 1965 and reviewed widely. Daniel Lerner lamented its lack of rigorous empirical work, saying that Ellul's most significant contribution was his "calamitous tone of voice," and noted that the book was more telling about the state of French sociology than it was about the phenomenon of propaganda.[3] On the other hand, Spanish sociologist E. J. Boneu praised Ellul's work as an important addition to the literature on propaganda, not because it did in fact add more data to the literature, but because it recast the discussion of propaganda according to novel themes and perspectives.[4]

---

2. Hitler, *Mein Kampf*, 180.
3. Lerner, review of *Propagandes*, 793–94.
4. Boneu, review of *Propagandes*, 338–39.

Nearly fifty years after its publication, the book continues to generate critical interaction in the fields of sociology and communication studies. To read Ellul's discussion of the origins and implications of propaganda in any technological society is to encounter a profound critique of our media-saturated world. Importantly, Ellul's argument turns on propaganda's capacities for turning individuals into collectives—the masses—suppressing individual freedom and autonomy. This concern, coupled with Ellul's argument that propaganda dampens spiritual sensitivity, proves a telling revelation of Ellul's commitment to individualism, which will be explored at greater length in chapter 7's examination of Ellul's ethics.

Propaganda: Its Purposes, Features, and Types

Ellul provides evidence of this concern for the making of the masses when he defines propaganda as "a set of methods employed by an organized group that wants to bring about the active or passive participation in its actions of a mass of individuals, psychologically unified through psychological manipulations and incorporated in an organization."[5] The section on propaganda in *The Technological Society* characterizes it as a human technique consisting of two fundamental parts: "a complex of mechanical techniques," by which Ellul means principally the mass media forms of "radio, press, and motion pictures" (and to which we might now add television, the Internet, and the cell phone), and "a complex of psychological (and even psychoanalytical) techniques which give access to exact knowledge of the human psyche."[6] The purpose of propaganda is to integrate human beings into a dehumanized world, to adapt them to the technological society.[7] Along with medicine, genetics, vocational counseling, and other techniques, propaganda is a tool aimed at helping humans be at home in and at peace with a world that is not made for them.[8]

In his foreword to *The Technological Society*, Robert Merton provides a preliminary glimpse of propaganda's necessity: "The technological society requires men to be content with what they are required to like; for those who are not content, it provides distractions—escape into absorption with

---

5. Ellul, *Propaganda*, 61.
6. Ellul, *Technological Society*, 363.
7. Ibid., 6.
8. Ibid., 22.

technically dominated media of popular culture and communication."[9] Propaganda, then, is media designed specifically to accommodate humanity to its new environment by synthesizing contentment or distraction. It does so by convincing people of the merits and virtues of their new milieu. As Ellul notes, submission to the demands of technique requires great effort on the part of the individual, and "this effort he could not make unless he was genuinely convinced, not merely constrained. He must be made to yield his heart and will, as he had yielded his body and brain . . . to the degree that material techniques became more precise, intellectual and psychic techniques became more necessary."[10]

As an integral aspect of technological society, propaganda is aimed primarily at "orthopraxis" rather than orthodoxy—at behavior consistent with the demands of technological society.[11] This, Ellul suggests, distinguishes contemporary propaganda from previous types of propaganda: "To view propaganda as still being what it was in 1850 is to cling to an obsolete concept of man and the means to influence him. . . . The aim of modern propaganda is no longer to modify ideas, but to provoke action."[12] According to Ellul, in order to provoke action, the propagandist must possess intimate knowledge of psychology, so that propaganda is a response to a latent desire or felt need.[13] In order to link individuals into a collective, the propagandist must be "familiar with collective sociological presuppositions, spontaneous myths, and broad ideologies,"[14] and he or she must use this knowledge to provide evidence that the promises of technological society are being fulfilled.

According to Ellul, propaganda has a curious relationship to reality. "It is well known," he writes, "that veracity and exactness are important elements in advertising" and that in the political realm as well, "there is no good reason to launch a propaganda campaign based on unbelievable or false facts."[15] Of course, this does not make propaganda true: "The lie is often suggested through techniques of *presentation, silence,*

---

9. Merton, foreword to *Technological Society*, viii.
10. Ellul, *Technological Society*, 115–16.
11. Ellul, *Propaganda*, 27.
12. Ibid., 25.
13. Ibid., 37.
14. Ibid., 38.
15. Ibid., 54.

and *innuendo*."[16] Those individuals who most trust their own abilities to distinguish between what is factually accurate and lies presented through omission, insinuation, or translation of context are the most susceptible to propaganda: "Anyone holding that conviction [that they can easily distinguish between the accurate and inaccurate] is extremely susceptible to propaganda because when propaganda does tell the 'truth,' he is then convinced that it is no longer propaganda; moreover, his self-confidence makes him all the more vulnerable to attacks of which he is unaware."[17] This admixture of the accurate and inaccurate, this interweaving of fact and misrepresentation, is used as a vehicle for provocation, as a "mechanism to slip from the facts, which would demand factual judgment, to moral terrain and to ethical judgment."[18] This movement toward uninformed or misinformed moral and ethical judgment is meant to generate certain behaviors through emotion—for example, indignation, "a tone which is almost always the mark of propaganda."[19]

Ellul differentiates between different types of propaganda. For example, he distinguishes between political propaganda and sociological propaganda. Political propaganda are those "techniques of influence employed by a government, a party, an administration, a pressure group, with a view to changing the behavior of the public."[20] Sociological propaganda is diverse, diffuse, and spontaneous, evident in advertising, technology, education, and social services, expressing the "the penetration of an ideology by means of its sociological context."[21] Many media of entertainment and amusement also conform to the characteristics of sociological propaganda. People learn from film and television what can be expected in their milieu and come to understand the norms of technological society; they "go to the movies to escape and consequently yield to [the pressures of technological society]. They find forgetfulness, and in forgetfulness the honied freedom they do not find in their work or at home. They live on screen a life they will never live in fact."[22] Media of entertainment and amusement can be sociological propaganda meant to reinforce a sense of contentment or freedom. In any case, propaganda of both

16. Ellul, *Propaganda*, 55–57.
17. Ibid., 52.
18. Ibid., 58.
19. Ibid.
20. Ibid., 62.
21. Ibid., 64.
22. Ellul, *Technological Society*, 377.

sorts—political and sociological—is mass-produced, mass-consumed, and aimed at "conformity of life."[23]

Ellul also distinguishes between agitation and integration. Propaganda of agitation is "most often subversive," bears "the stamp of opposition," and is "led by a party seeking to destroy the government or the established order. It seeks rebellion or war."[24] Because it starts with a marginal group and spreads, Ellul also uses the synonymous term *horizontal propaganda* to describe this type. It is effective in galvanizing people who have a grievance with the existing order of things and in promoting their conformity to alternative or subversive norms. Integration stands in stark contrast to agitation and is "the propaganda of developed nations and characteristic of our civilization . . . [it] aims at stabilizing the social body, at unifying and reinforcing it. It is thus the preferred instrument of government, though properly speaking it is not exclusively political propaganda."[25] This is the propaganda that comes from the top down, and is thus also called by the synonymous term *vertical propaganda*.

The Spiritual Effects of Propaganda

One of Ellul's chief concerns with propaganda was its effect upon spiritual and ecclesial life, as evidenced by a section of *Propaganda* devoted to the effects of propaganda upon the church. In *The Technological Society*, Ellul refers to the earliest known use of the term *propaganda*, calling it a "spiritual technique" used by the church along with other techniques such as aid to the helpless and indigent. In 1622, Pope Gregory the XV founded the *Congregatio de Propaganda Fide*. This "Congregation for Propagating the Faith" was a committee of cardinals designated to supervise the expansion of Christianity by missionaries sent to non-Christian countries. Religiously, this was understood as a natural and beneficial outgrowth of the so-called Great Commission given in Scripture:

> Then Jesus came to them and said, "All authority in heaven and on earth has been given to me. Therefore go and make disciples of all nations, baptizing them in the name of the Father and of the Son and of the Holy Spirit, and teaching them to obey everything

---

23. Ellul, *Propaganda*, 68.
24. Ibid., 71.
25. Ibid., 75.

I have commanded you. And surely I am with you always, to the very end of the age.[26]

While the term *propaganda* originally connoted the propagation of the faith, according to Ellul, the effects of contemporary propaganda upon the church are spiritually debilitating. Propaganda, through provocation with the aim of action consonant with the demands of technological society, tends to divorce belief and behavior. It has this effect upon Christian and non-Christian alike. As Ellul wrote, "Obviously, church members are caught in the net of propaganda and react pretty much like everyone else. As a result, an almost complete dissociation takes place between their Christianity and their behavior. Their Christianity remains a spiritual and purely internal thing."[27] A "systematic widening" of this gap is the result of propaganda, both in the public and private domains.[28] According to Ellul, this coupling of Christian belief, on the one hand, and behavior consonant with the demands of technological society, on the other hand, "makes the propagation of Christianity increasingly difficult. The psychological structures built by propaganda are not propitious to Christian beliefs."[29] Propaganda becomes one means that militates against the presence of the kingdom, or Christian "presence in the modern world."

Churches, and not just individual Christians, are faced with a new dilemma vis-à-vis contemporary propaganda. According to Ellul, churches must choose between two unpleasant alternatives:

> *Either not to make propaganda*—but then, while the churches slowly and carefully win a man to Christianity, the mass media quickly mobilize the masses, and churchmen gain the impression of being "out of step," on the fringes of history, and without power to change a thing. *Or to make propaganda*— this dilemma is surely one of the most cruel with which the churches are faced at present. For it seems that people manipulated by propaganda become increasingly impervious to spiritual realities, less and less suited for the autonomy of the Christian life. We are seeing a considerable religious transformation, by which the religious element, through

---

26. Matt 28:18–20.
27. Ellul, *Propaganda*, 228.
28. Ibid.
29. Ibid., 229.

the means of the myth, is being absorbed little by little by propaganda and becoming one of its categories.[30]

Despite the tragic aspect of the dilemma—the fact that either choice has a distinct downside—Ellul argues that churches should not make or use propaganda: "In fact, what happens as soon as the church avails itself of propaganda is a reduction of Christianity to the level of all other ideologies or secular religions."[31] He then repeats this more forcefully by claiming that "from the moment the church uses propaganda and uses it successfully, it becomes, unremittingly, a purely sociological institution."[32]

In his analysis of the consequences of propaganda used by the church, Ellul foreshadows the media ecology discipline (for whom he is now a canonical figure), emphasizing the importance of both form and content and suggesting that the medium may become the message:

> When the church uses propaganda, it always tries to justify itself in one of two ways: It says, first of all, that it puts these efficient media in the service of Jesus Christ. But if one reflects for a moment, one realizes that this means nothing. What is in the service of Jesus Christ receives its character and effectiveness from Jesus Christ . . . In fact, a statement by the church that it is placing the media at the service of Christ, is not a logical or ethical explanation, but a pious formula without content.[33]

For Ellul, a church that uses propaganda—a constellation of psychological and material techniques for manipulating behavior—preaches, the power of propaganda, the effectiveness of the medium, rather than the supremacy of God in Christ. This exchange of truth for power leads to the de-Christianization of the church.

> At the end of this brief analysis we can conclude that propaganda is one of the most powerful factors of de-Christianization in the world through the psychological modifications that it effects, through the ideological morass with which it has flooded the consciousness of the masses, through the reduction of Christianity to the level of an ideology, through the never-ending temptation

---

30. Ibid.

31. Ibid., 230.

32. Ibid. Because Ellul interpreted many post-War Protestant practices of mass evangelism as using the techniques of propaganda, he was critical of American preacher Billy Graham. See Ellul, *Humiliation of the Word*, 202; Ellul, *New Demons*, 154, 216.

33. Ellul, *Propaganda*, 231.

held out to the church—all this is the creation of a mental universe foreign to Christianity. And this de-Christianization through the effects of one instrument—propaganda—is much greater than through all the anti-Christian doctrines.[34]

Here Ellul points implicitly to the chief irony of propaganda: that the term *propaganda* has come full circle, from signifying the very means of propagating the Christian faith to signifying a barrier to doing so.

Humiliation of the Word: Hearing and Seeing, Word and Image

The philosophical and theological reasons that undergird Ellul's analysis of propaganda are spelled out thoroughly in *The Humiliation of the Word*, which appeared in English in 1985. It is one of those rare works by Ellul in which he combines his sociological and theological analyses. Again we find that his considerations about a major issue in the modern world are grounded in his Christian view of what it means to be a human being. Communication is a fundamental concern to Ellul because we have been made what might be called "communicative creatures" by our Creator. For Ellul, what distinguishes human beings from nonhuman creatures is speech. He writes, "God creates human beings as speaking beings. Perhaps this is one of the meanings of the image of God: one who responds and is responsible; a counterpart who will dialogue, who is both at a certain distance and has the ability to communicate."[35] Here we encounter two of Ellul's driving ideas—the inherently *relational* nature of human beings and the essentially *dialogical* nature of human speech. He emphasizes the extent to which a person's words are a profound expression of their being, such that words "belong" to persons in a quite literal way. Words separated from the person who uttered them are dangerously open to distortion or misunderstanding. Decontextualized words, divorced from their originator, are especially prone to reduction to the empty slogans of propaganda. Positively, as deeply personal expressions, human words make possible genuine relationship with others and with God.

In stressing the importance of speech and words in this way, human beings are understood to be like God, who is distinguished from all rival

---

34. Ibid., 231–32.
35. Ellul, *Humiliation of the Word*, 63.

gods by a capacity for speech. Ellul writes that "human speech is invested with unlimited importance because God chose the word as his means."[36] As we will see, the reference to "unlimited importance" is hardly overstated, if Ellul's analysis is correct. A characteristic mark of the biblical God is that he is a God who speaks his divine Word. For Ellul's account, it is critically important that God speaks the world into existence: "God said, Let there be light" (Gen 1:3). Creation is depicted as the product of God's direct and unrivaled agency forming the cosmos through the spoken word. The act of creation sets the paradigm for all God's action in the world, which takes place through his sovereign, revealed Word. God speaks not only in creation, but speaks continually to his people, providing guidance and instruction, appointing spokespeople to speak on his behalf (such as the Old Testament prophets), and revealing himself supremely through Jesus Christ as the Incarnate Word of God (John 1:1–18).

Ellul draws an implication about the primacy of speech and words from this theological framework that proves decisive for his thinking about human communication in all its facets, including propaganda. He asserts that "the only possible relationship with God is based on the word, and nothing else. This is because the biblical God speaks, and does nothing else. . . . In the sphere of truth, everything is related to the word, nothing to sight."[37] We need to notice that Ellul is not simply claiming divinely revealed Truth is known only through God's Word. That would be a fairly conventional claim for someone within Ellul's Protestant tradition. Rather, Ellul is extending the logic of a theological claim in order to draw a more general theoretical conclusion. He argues that in the "sphere of truth" or what he elsewhere calls "the order of truth" in general—not simply in the matter of Divine Truth—everything depends on the word. Here Ellul refers to "word" rather than "Word." This is an important distinction. The term *word* refers to words and speech; *Word* refers to God's revelation, to Scripture, and especially to Jesus Christ as Word of God. Thus, Ellul's theologically based contention is that the human pursuit of truth is a matter of words and hearing, not images and seeing. Sight cannot be the avenue to genuine truth about the world, let alone to Divine Truth.

Ellul backs up this interpretive stance by arguing that the biblical text gives primacy to hearing over seeing. Proclamation by spoken word is the normative means of God's communication rather than manifestation by

---

36. Ibid., 65.
37. Ibid., 71.

deeds or appearances. Ellul believes that miraculous events mentioned in the Bible are merely visible "signs" that "have no meaning in themselves." He argues that "the sign must always be explained. What matters is the word that gives meaning to what is seen."[38] From the standpoint of divine revelation, argues Ellul, the "decisive issue is not to have seen something, but to hear a word which is utterly clear, distinct, and explicit, and contains a revelation, a promise, and a mission altogether. This is a denial of all possibility of knowledge through sight, which places sight and language in contradiction with each other."[39] This stark opposition of hearing and seeing, and therefore between words and images, means that Scripture's teaching about the subjective experience of personal faith in God is oriented with reference to what is heard rather than seen. Therefore the quest for verifiable evidence to prove the claims of faith should not be encouraged. A well-known New Testament episode that is consistent with Ellul's instinct is when the character known as "Doubting Thomas" demands tangible, physical evidence to verify the identity of the risen Christ, who then announces, "blessed are those who have not seen and yet have believed" (John 20:24–29). Certain interpretations of the fall also resonate with Ellul's position: Adam and Eve refused to take God's word regarding the fruit of the Tree of the Knowledge of Good and Evil, allowing the serpent to twist God's words by showing them that the fruit was good to eat and would make them like God; Adam and Eve chose by sight, rather than according to what they had heard from God. For Ellul, this has been the way of the fallen world—to say "seeing is believing"—while the way of faith is to say "hearing is believing." It is the human refusal to be satisfied with revealed words, and its subsequent quest for visible images to represent the divine, that leads humanity into idolatry. Ellul's acute sensitivity to the issue of idolatry reveals his deep roots in the Reformed tradition of Protestant Christianity. Although Ellul generally was unenthusiastic about John Calvin's theology, nevertheless Ellul's perspective is basically consistent with the teachings of Calvin and seventeenth-century Puritans who strongly emphasized that images were idolatrous and therefore rejected visual representations in churches.[40]

38. Ibid., 74.
39. Ibid.
40. For more, see Goddard, "Jacques Ellul on Idolatry."

The Dominance of Images

Examining the communication patterns of the modern world from the standpoint of the primacy of hearing and the supreme value of words, Ellul is deeply distressed. He believes that the word has been "humiliated"—degraded, disrespected, and dethroned. On every front, he recognizes that visual images rather than words dominate the Western technological society.

According to his analysis, the dominance of technique is responsible for the primacy of seeing. "All techniques are based on visualization and involve visualization. If a phenomenon cannot be transformed into something visual, it cannot be the object of a technique."[41] As with *Propaganda*, we see in *The Humiliation of the Word* that Ellul's subsequent writings have extended his insights that were first laid out in *The Technological Society*. Technique is accompanied by an image-saturated society: "Images today are the daily nutrient of our sensory experience, our thought processes, our feelings, and our ideology."[42] Ellul contends that the triumph of sight and the accompanying regression of words mean that human beings live in a social environment shaped decisively by the ubiquity of photographs, films, television, advertising, billboards, road signs and other means, and he believes that the "omnipresence of images . . . is not an accidental, sporadic, changeable fact. We are dealing instead with an almost total milieu in which all of existence unfolds more or less smoothly. Truly it is a *universe* of images in the midst of which we are set as spectators."[43] In this situation, reliance upon images comes naturally and easily. Because they are socially valued so strongly, images are considered trustworthy, while words are suspect: "Whenever we remain without images, information seems dubious to us in our day."[44]

Ellul openly laments this "unconditional victory of the visual and images" and their "triumphant march" toward a "spectacle-oriented" society, which has consequences at both the individual and collective levels. He describes the "image-oriented person" as someone with a worrying set of mental habits and social values: "Western people no longer hear; everything is grasped by sight. They no longer speak; they show."[45] Ellul offers a

---

41. Ellul, *Humiliation of the Word*, 11.
42. Ibid., 1.
43. Ibid., 126. Italics in original.
44. Ibid., 114.
45. Ibid., 204.

philosophical analysis of image-based thinking as "thought by association and suggestion," that is, by an association of images rather than ideas; as "a purely emotional stage of thinking"; as dependent upon "violent visual impact if thought is to be set in motion"; and geared toward enabling people to "grasp facts in an overall manner. It is thus a matter of intuition."[46] Ellul is concerned for the reliance upon an "instantaneous intuition" involving "a kind of direct communication of knowledge, as if it did not pass through the brain, as if reason were absent and intelligence had nothing to do with it."[47] For example, Ellul bemoans the widespread use of charts, graphs, and statistics in public life, which are presented as "facts" and "proofs" without discussion, yet which depend critically upon interpretation and explanation. Images are geared toward the transmission of data and facts, typically taken at face value as conveying accurately what they portray. This is not to say that charts, graphs, and figures cannot convey information consonant with truth and accessible to reason, but that they promote a culture in which the possession and use of such images blunts reason through an appeal to the authority of the image itself.

What bothers Ellul most is the dominance of an unreasonable form of reasoning: "the image that creates this thinking gives rise to a feeling of evidence and a conviction that is not based on reason" since "obviously you cannot dispute with an image . . . What produces immediate assent cannot bear the discussion process."[48] This assent is geared toward an immediate reaction and response, not a measured dialogue or time-consuming discussion. One of Ellul's biggest concerns with the dominance of images is the eclipse of reason itself, especially its expression as critical inquiry. The person who thinks with images

> resists demonstrations. Reasoning irritates and exasperates him without convincing him: what good are such roundabout methods? Why such a slow pace? Why stop at every step to secure one's position, when he can have the result in one move? Intuition can enable him to grasp the totality in a flash. The most precise demonstration possible will not convince such a person, because he is desensitized to reason. The sequence of the parts of a reasoned argument does not strike him as at all necessary.[49]

46. Ellul, *Humiliation of the Word*, 210–11.
47. Ibid., 211.
48. Ibid., 213.
49. Ibid., 216.

For those who are oriented to images, "the words seem like wind, or like something without life."[50] Ellul claims, rather gloomily, that "the problem is not just a genuine inability to think in the two modes, a necessary exclusion of each by the other. It is also a genuine refusal to use both forms of thought."[51] Those oriented toward images and those toward words show "only scorn and distrust for the other."[52]

On the other hand, the word is associated with the domain of truth. The word "necessarily gives rise to a mode of thought by demonstration, following a logical or dialectical process." The key assumption is that "reasoned argument is convincing" because it provides "demonstration" and "rational proof" rather than an emotional basis. For word-oriented people, intuition is questionable and images are dubious: "always suspect . . . at best they are accessories that have no meaning apart from the explanations that accompany them."[53] Persuasion through images is, according to Ellul, "the opposite of demonstration; intuition is the opposite of reasoning; and the association of ideas excludes any possibility of the rigor of logical thought."[54] What is at stake for Ellul is nothing less than the demise of the habits of logical thought altogether, which in turn creates the social conditions wherein propaganda can triumph. Alternatively, regard for the word is key to the triumph of genuine human existence. The word "is the means of human relationship and dialogue, which is the dialectical exercise of experience."[55] Again we see Ellul's concern for the presence of truly human interactions in a technological society.

According to Ellul, the basis of this polarization between two conflicting modes of thought is profoundly deep: "We must not think that a person is absolutely free to play both games at once, to use two instruments equally, because they condition the whole person so profoundly. We are modified by our own means of expression, and the dominant use of one means prevents our valid use of the other."[56] If human beings are "modified" at the level of their "whole person" by the attitudes and outlook conditioned by the basic patterns of the image or the patterns of the word, then what is

---

50. Ellul, *Humiliation of the Word*, 217.
51. Ibid.
52. Ibid.
53. Ibid., 216.
54. Ibid., 217.
55. Ibid., 215–16.
56. Ibid., 217.

at stake is nothing less than an erosion of our most characteristic human capacity—the ability for speech, for dialogue and discourse that leads to understanding of truth and meaning.

Ellul explains that the triumph of the image does not mean that no one uses words anymore; it means that words are only marginally significant and find their place only within the universe of images. Accordingly,

> Images are the chosen form of expression in our civilization—images, not words. For though our era speaks, and abounds in printed paper, so that written thought has never been as widespread as today, still there is a strange movement that deprives the word of its importance. Talk and newspapers are like word mills to which no one attaches any importance anymore. Who would still consider a book as something decisive and capable of changing his life, when there are so many of them? And a person's word, buried under the flood of millions of people's words, no longer has any meaning or outreach.[57]

In this context Ellul points out the seemingly inevitable reduction of words to mere slogans, which then become the central content of propaganda:

> In slogans, words are completely stripped of their reasonable and meaningful content. All oral propaganda rests on the fact that language loses its meaning and retains only the power of inciting and triggering. The word has become mere sound: pure nervous excitation, to which people respond by reflex, or because of group pressure. If a speaker fails to make use of the magic words which automatically stir up hatreds, passions, mobs, devotion, and curses, the rest of his language dissolves, as far as his listeners are concerned, into a gush of lava, an overflow of monotony, a contemptible fog that prevents or smothers action. The word thus loses its power.[58]

This is a sobering analysis, especially considering that Ellul's French version appeared in 1981, just one year after CNN was established as the first twenty-four-hour television news channel, and long before the ascendency of digital media. It would seem that Ellul's concerns for the "humiliation" of the word should be redoubled in our era of PowerPoint, 24/7 talk radio, MTV, YouTube, mobile phones (used more as hyper-portable screens than telephones), and Twitter (with its reduction of speech to 140 characters).

57. Ellul, *Humiliation of the Word*, 126–27.
58. Ibid., 127.

Reality and Truth

Ellul adds to the distinction between image and word another important distinction: that between reality and truth. Reality correlates with images and sight; truth correlates with words and hearing. Reality and truth are interpreted as opposing "domains" or "orders" that operate on the basis of different modes of knowing.

"Reality is what is seen, counted, and quantified, and is located in space."[59] Its orientation is the material world, and what can be known about it by accumulating data through empirical investigation. In this realm, facts are considered decisive. Ellul believes that

> for today's individual a fact is the ultimate reason, the supreme value, and an unimpeachable proof. Everything bows before a fact. We must obey it. We are irrational, idealistic dreamers if we do not trust facts. It is not enough to take facts into account; we also attribute decisive value to them. No justice, truth, or humanity can stand up in the face of a fact. It decides everything.[60]

He continues: "This collective submission to facts that have been transformed into values and this frenzy of wanting to know nothing but the reality of facts—these attitudes contain within them what we are seeing in our society: the triumph of things material."[61] Ellul's analysis is that the modern world has created a small and closed universe where only what can be seen—albeit with the naked eye or on a television screen, or perhaps using a telescope or microscope—has validity and importance. Only reality matters, and reality is transmitted through images that "can in no way convey anything at all about the order of truth": "It never grasps anything but an appearance or outward behavior. It is unable to convey a spiritual experience, a requirement of justice, a testimony to the deepest feelings of a person, or to bear witness to the truth."[62] Ellul is disturbed that modern society is oriented by, and apparently satisfied with, "the triumph of reality." He laments that "we bestow dignity, authenticity, and spiritual truth" on what is merely reality—what can be seen, touched, and tasted. "We enclose within the image everything that belongs to the order of truth."[63] Ellul attri-

---

59. Ellul, *Humiliation of the Word*, 10n3.
60. Ibid., 137.
61. Ibid., 137–38.
62. Ibid., 29.
63. Ibid., 95.

butes much of this doleful situation to the role of science in creating the assumption of a closed, materialistic universe; science "has finally convinced people that the only possible truth consists in knowing reality."[64] To return to some of Ellul's central categories, reality deals only with means (questions about how things work) and is understood and conveyed through images, while truth deals with ends (questions about purpose and meaning) and is understood and conveyed through words. The "word is the creator, founder, and producer of truth . . . nothing besides language can reach or establish the order of truth."[65]

The denigration of the word and of truth is the denigration of human meaning and experience. Since language is the specific distinctiveness of human beings, it is natural that truth can be pursued and grasped through language. For Ellul, the order of truth operates through the expression of dialogue, debate, and critical reflection—all of which require words. The erosion of critical thinking is at the heart of Ellul's dismay with technique's focus on reality. He writes, "The habit of living in this image-oriented world leads me to give up dialectical thought and criticism. It is so much easier to give up and let myself be carried along by the continually renewed wave of images."[66] For Ellul, an orientation to truth through the word is time-consuming and difficult; acceptance of reality on the basis of images is quick and easy. He argues that "discourse implies a long process: an indirect approach and a kind of winding movement involving successive approximations that irritate lazy modern people. Visual representation is the easy, efficient, quick path."[67] For example, a child's education is increasingly organized around images, with teaching expressing what is to be known "in a picture, a diagram, or a reproduction. Oral explanations overwhelm and tire the listener; words no longer hold people's attention or their interest. Knowledge today is expressed through images."[68] The order of truth is undermined by vapid speech: "The habit of speaking without saying anything has eaten away at the word like a cancer."[69]

The consequences of the modern preference for reality over truth are profound. People have become "utterly indifferent to the question of truth,"

64. Ellul, *Humiliation of the Word*, 31.
65. Ibid., 23.
66. Ibid., 28.
67. Ibid., 133.
68. Ibid., 131.
69. Ibid., 155.

which includes an indifference to "their destiny and the meaning of life."[70] Like other critics of modernity, Ellul decries the way in which "all modern thought tries to imprison us within this reality and nothing else. Modern thought tries to make us consider reality as truth—the only truth, truth itself. Truth verifiable by science. Truth constructed within reality. The truth of Marxism founded on reality alone. Reality as the criterion of the true, the good, the just."[71] At bottom, this is a profound mistake. Ellul writes:

> Our civilization's major temptation (a problem that comes from technique's preponderant influence) is to confuse reality with truth. We are made to believe that reality is truth: the only truth . . . We think that truth is contained within reality and expressed by it. Nothing more. Moreover, there is nothing left beyond reality any more. Nothing is Other; the Wholly Other no longer exists. Everything is reduced to this verifiable reality which is scientifically measurable and pragmatically modifiable.[72]

Iconoclasm: Resisting the Image, Salvaging the Word

Ellul sums up the foregoing analysis by saying, "through the eruption of unlimited artificial images, we have reduced truth to the order of reality and banished the shy and fleeting expression of truth."[73] This situation creates an existential crisis for modern life, circumstances that Ellul calls "intolerable" because they produce "acute suffering and panic: a person cannot live deprived of truth and situated in fiction. He does not know exactly what makes him suffer, but despairing to be when he has no real being, he lives with a latent panic and an unconscious vanity. He must find a way out at all costs; he must restore truth."[74] In short: "Without the word, human life is hell."[75] Ellul even states that humanity's future is in grave jeopardy: "Anyone wishing to save humanity today must first of all save the word."[76] But how? If people are so profoundly conditioned by the dominance of the image and

---

70. Ibid., 201.
71. Ibid., 182. Ellul shares a number of central concerns expressed at around the same time by Lesslie Newbigin. See *Foolishness to the Greeks*, especially ch. 4.
72. Ellul, *Humiliation of the Word*, 27.
73. Ibid., 228.
74. Ibid.
75. Ibid., 230.
76. Ibid., 254.

are satisfied with the humiliation of the word, which alone can lead to truth, how can truth and meaning be found in a "rational, positivistic, scientific world" oriented by the "gods of consumerism, power, and machines?"[77]

Turning to theological considerations, Ellul offers hope in the Bible's picture of an ultimate reconciliation between word and image, between reality and truth—actually, in the "eschatological" truth that is revealed only at the consummation of human history by God's final actions of judgment and salvation. It is important to note that Ellul believed that truth and reality corresponded one to the other in the prelapsarian state and that the fall had divorced the two. It is likewise important to note that Ellul's Christocentric theology provides the basis for an eventual reunion of reality and truth that is found only in Christ, who is the agent of "the reconciliation between image and word, between reality and truth, as the end point and the metahistorical moment reached after the historical process of contradiction."[78] Ellul emphasizes that this reconciliation cannot be brought about by human instrumentality; in the course of history, such a synthesis is impossible. But, with his characteristic emphasis on enacting one's faith with confidence in God's ultimate purposes, Ellul insists that "this relationship can be lived only in the integrity of contradiction and in the hope of reconciliation. But it must always be a present hope: a hope that changes the situation now."[79] For Ellul, God's final triumph, which unites word and image, is "assured, absolutely certain" by faith, even if it is "not yet visible or accomplished." Although he does not say so explicitly, it seems clear that Ellul believes that only Christians—because of "the company of him who consummates this reconciliation"[80]—are capable of offering the right sort of resistance to the idolatry of visual images and restoring the word to its rightful place of primacy in Western culture.

What specific steps does Ellul advocate? "What we must do in this time and place, based on the certainty of reconciliation, is to hear the command to iconoclasm, which resounds continually."[81] Literally, the term *iconoclasm* is derived from the Greek word for image breaking. Ellul's rhetoric plays on the term also to refer to the necessity of destroying the hegemony of images in Western culture, which will involve challenging and upsetting the cher-

---

77. Ellul, *Humiliation of the Word*, 228.
78. Ibid., 254.
79. Ibid.
80. Ibid., 255.
81. Ibid.

ished beliefs and assumptions that are popularly held. In the concluding pages of *The Humiliation of the Word*, Ellul offers some specific steps of active resistance.

First, "we must commit ourselves continually to this difficult eviction of images from the domain of truth. They must remain what they are: useful, unexcelled means for reality and action, good for this realm. But they must not claim to go beyond this, not claim to evict the word, not lead people into worshipping images."[82] Positively, Ellul accepts that images can have their appropriate place: "we do not attack images when they are reduced to their proper level, function and role."[83] The problem is when images are assumed to be adequate in the "domain of truth." In this context Ellul's language of worship and idolatry needs to be taken seriously. To borrow language from St. Augustine, Ellul's point is that images can be used, but should never be loved. Images are improper objects of full allegiance, loyalty, and adulation before which we submit ourselves—all this is "religious" behavior. Resisting such misplaced homage means speaking out to "attack" the dominance of audiovisual technologies, especially computers; he refers to audiovisuals as an "appalling antihuman war machine."[84] The dehumanizing effect of technological dependence is his constant concern. He refers to computers as "pretentious devices that arrogantly substitute themselves for the word and for reason."[85]

Iconoclastic resistance also includes the need to "attack all abusive scientism, everything that tries to pass itself off as truth, except for the word, which is characterized by chiaroscuro and hesitation. It is filled with meaning and is evocative and provocative."[86] Ellul makes clear that his objection to "scientism" does not involve an objection "to science as such, but only to its idolatrous pretension to be exclusive, substitutive, and reductionist."[87] The root issue is when science "pretends to be the whole truth by limiting and excluding everything that goes beyond it." For example, taking Ellul's point does not compel us to reject the use of medical imaging technologies simply because computers are involved in generating the relevant scientific

---

82. Ibid., 256.
83. Ibid., 259.
84. Ibid., 257.
85. Ibid., 258.
86. Ibid. Ellul's reference to chiaroscuro is an allusion to the subtle shadings or nuances that are possible with the careful use of words.
87. Ibid.

data. His point is that automatic acceptance of "the computer says" as the "ultimate reason" for a particular course of response and decision about medical treatment is a dangerously reductionist tactic that neglects the place of existential, rational, and moral judgments made by human beings.

Importantly, Ellul's iconoclastic strategy also includes an insistence on the "necessity of comprehensible language. Language is made to be heard and understood. Language brings the word to us."[88] Ellul has in mind the way in which Christians "must challenge energetically all the snares and temptations of mysterious, mystical, delirious, and fiery language. In the world as it is today, the recourse to such language amounts to surrender and betrayal of humanity."[89] This insight—that Christians have a special duty to puncture inflated rhetoric and to restore moderation to public debate—is a key part of his understanding of the Christian contribution to politics, as chapter 5 in this book will show. For Ellul, "speaking clearly and reasonably expresses love of neighbor."[90] Here we see a concern for language to be used according to its original intention, namely, for the sake of human relationship, and especially to overcome isolation and alienation. The use of meaningful, measured, and understandable language is enormously important for Ellul as a major step to resist the "technicalization of relationships."[91]

Because Ellul never considered his ideas to be the "last word" on any topic (nor did he wish them to be so considered), and because he distrusted the technicization of resistance, he rarely offered specific and concrete advice about our response to the problems of communication in a technological society. He considered his own speech and writing dialogical, intended to generate an exchange of ideas, to spark debate, and to prompt new questions rather than to offer answers; he aimed to set his readers off on an adventure, in imitation of his hero, Karl Barth. That said, in these matters Ellul's reflections are stronger in their diagnosis and critique than in their articulation of responses and viable alternatives. As with other prophets, he is better at tearing down than building up. Like David Gill, we are impressed by Ellul's critique, yet wish that he had developed more concrete alternatives to exemplify the practical steps involved in meaningful "iconoclastic" practices.

88. Ellul, *Humiliation of the Word*, 260.
89. Ibid., 261.
90. Ibid., 262.
91. Ibid.

Despite this shortcoming, Ellul's interpretation of communication in the modern world shows why Gill has claimed that "few, if any, Christian intellectuals of this era have developed as sophisticated and powerful a critique of contemporary civilization as Jacques Ellul."[92] In some ways, Ellul's appraisal of propaganda was an urgently needed product of his times, as the unspeakable horror done by Nazi tactics demanded a detailed and strong response. But in other ways, Ellul's analysis of the ascendency of the image and the demise of the word, and with it the loss of rational reflection in public and private life, was a prophetic word that seems well ahead of his times. In our media-saturated epoch, Ellul's warnings about a technological mindset that threatens to eclipse our fundamental humanity deserve fresh examination. They should occasion a reappraisal of and renewed debate about the deeper implications and human costs of rapid "advances" in the thorough digitalization of life.

---

92. Gill, "Jacques Ellul and Francis Schaeffer," 34.

CHAPTER 4

The City and Urbanism

> *"The city is man's greatest work. It is his great attempt to attain autonomy, to exercise will and intelligence. This is where all his efforts are concentrated, where all his powers are born. No other of man's works, technical or philosophical, is equivalent to the city. . . . All of his works are secondary to the city. Just as Jesus Christ is God's greatest work, so we can say, with all the consequences of such a statement, that the city is man's greatest work."*[1]

THE TWENTIETH CENTURY WAS the century of urbanization. When Jacques Ellul was born, 175 million people—approximately 10 percent of the world's population—lived in urban areas. By the time World War II was over, the percentage had nearly tripled; about 750 million people lived in cities. By 1970, just a quarter of a century later, that number had nearly doubled, swelling to almost 1.5 billion. In the course of only seventy years, the number of urbanites had grown by nearly an order of magnitude.

Not only had the number of city dwellers grown, but the size of cities had also increased dramatically. In 1900, London was the largest city in the world, with a population of 6.5 million, about the size of present-day Chennai, India. At that time, all of the world's ten most populous cities were in Europe or North America, and none had more than 10 million inhabitants. By 1950, New York City had surpassed the 10 million mark, becoming the first megacity.

---

1. Ellul, *Meaning of the City*, 154.

The City and Urbanism

Urbanization had been on the rise since industrialization began in earnest in the late 1700s. Before the industrial era, cities grew because their walls provided security and their proximity to transportation routes provided opportunities for trade. Beginning with the industrial era, cities also grew because they concentrated capital and wage labor, providing unparalleled possibilities for economic growth. For this reason, they also concentrated hopeful but impoverished masses migrating from largely agricultural hinterlands. Some people moved to cities because of the pull of upward mobility. Others were displaced as their lands were "enclosed"—land previously inhabited and worked as common areas transitioned to private property as feudalism drew its final breaths—or because developments in agricultural technology put them out of work.

Common to industrial cities, whether of the north or the south, were Dickensian scenes of squalor and oppression. By the middle of the twentieth century, the city had taken on a new role in public consciousness. The 1927 German expressionist film *Metropolis*[2] captured this consciousness with a dystopian vision of oppressive labor conditions, tenement housing, class conflict, and political upheaval. The late 1960s made *Metropolis* seem simultaneously prescient and understated, as cities across the globe were primary sites of class conflict, violent political unrest, and student-led protest movements.

Responses to the profound social changes accompanying urbanization were mixed, especially among urban planners and futurists. Some followed in the utopian tradition of Ebenezer Howard, who had envisioned "Garden Cities,"[3] settlements that would unite the best of the city and the best of the countryside. Others, such as Charles-Edouard Jeanneret (1887–1965), better known as Le Corbusier, advocated planning and architecture as ambitious and mechanical as industrialism itself, noting that houses were simply machines for living.[4] The contributions of planners were accompanied by the work of Jane Jacobs (1916–2006) and Lewis Mumford (1895–1990), regarded by many as the two greatest urbanists of the twentieth century. Jacobs' *The Death and Life of Great American Cities*, a critique of modernist planners such as Le Corbusier and Robert Moses, found hope in the diversity and density of cities.[5] Mumford, in *The City in History*, which won the

---

2. Lang, *Metropolis*.
3. Howard, *Garden Cities*.
4. Le Corbusier, *The City of To-Morrow*.
5. Jacobs, *Death and Life*.

National Book Award, argued that cities were doomed to death and destruction unless they began to organize themselves around the needs of human beings rather than around the needs of machines.[6] In fact, Mumford argued that the plight of cities was essentially a religious one. Cities had always been planned around places of worship—temples, for example—which had controlled the organization of space and activities in the urban landscapes. Mumford argued that worship still controlled the organization of cities, but that we had begun to worship the machine, organizing our lives around industrial and transportation practices that were neither humanly scaled nor environmentally benign. Instead of organizing cities to serve the idol of the machine, Mumford argued that we should organize them in such a way as reflects our worship of the human being. Only such religious devotion to humanism could change the city's trajectory toward destruction. These religious associations had become common to thinking about the city. In 1927, *Metropolis* included a famous scene in which oppressed workers whose drudgery is required to make urban life possible are sacrificed to the "Moloch" machine. Nearly thirty years later, Alan Ginsberg, writing in New York City, published what became a famous poem, "Howl," the second part of which describes the urban industrial world as Moloch, a god demanding human sacrifice.[7]

If even the secular debates about cities had taken on religious overtones, it should come as no surprise that theologians, too, were following closely the developments in urbanism and, along with the best of the Christian tradition, providing commentary that took the city seriously. The city was common as an object of inquiry in its own right and, just as with the pattern set by Augustine, was also common as a trope or heuristic device.[8] The year 1965 saw the publication of Harvey Cox's book *The Secular City: Secularization and Urbanization in Theological Perspective*, a challenge to the anti-urban bias of much American Protestantism.[9] The late 1960s also saw the publication of Francis Schaeffer's *Death in the City*, a collection of lectures given at Wheaton College just five months after race riots shook Chicago to its core in the wake of the assassination of Martin Luther King Jr. in Memphis, Tennessee.[10] While "city," for Schaeffer, means more than

6. Mumford, *The City in History*.
7. Ginsberg, "Howl."
8. Augustine, *City of God*.
9. Cox, *The Secular City*.
10. Schaeffer, *Death in the City*.

just an urban area, the core of its argument is captured at the end of the first chapter: "Because man has turned from God, there are hungers on every side, there is death in the *polis, there is death in the city!*"[11]

The Meaning of the City: Its Reception

It was in this context of demographic shift, social turmoil, and scholarly ambivalence that Jacques Ellul wrote his book *The Meaning of the City*, published in 1970.[12] Ellul had realized the singular importance for the late twentieth century of the city as a form of human settlement: "We are in the city, and this is one of the most important facts of our generation. It is absolutely indispensable that we realize what this means for us, for our actual life: The undeniable presence and influence of the city are of infinitely greater importance than the urban problem in itself."[13] This realization had begun much earlier, as Ellul considered the widespread origins and implications of technological society for human community and noted the rise of urban planning as a technique—the one best way to organize human settlements.[14]

The Meaning of the City was one of very few Ellul works published first in English. With this work, Ellul was speaking into the world of Cox, Jacobs, Mumford, and others, and doing it in their own language. The book was supposed to be the contribution of a world-famous public intellectual to a pressing matter. *The Technological Society* had already made a considerable impact, and readers were prepared to hear Ellul's voice on one of the most pressing issues of the day.

As would be expected, *The Meaning of the City* was widely read and reviewed by scholars in multiple disciplines. Activist, legal scholar, and lay theologian William Stringfellow received the book with praise. Cox, writing in a Roman Catholic journal, *Commonweal*, commended the book to his readers, noting that "Jacques Ellul is neither a purblind Luddite nor a quaint religious fanatic. Though his theology has some serious thin spots and even some holes here and there, his instincts are usually dependable. He cannot be ignored."[15] Despite a warm reception by some, it is fair to

---

11. Ibid., 21.
12. Ellul, *Meaning of the City*.
13. Ibid., 147.
14. See, for example, Ellul, *Technological Society*, 4, 111.
15. Cox, review of *Meaning of the City*, 357.

say that the book was widely condemned. Theologians and social scientists alike rejected what they took to be Ellul's methods and his conclusions. Theologian Gibson Winter wrote that Ellul "interpreted the city in the Bible through the 'heavenly Jerusalem' in a bald and unrelieved fashion," the result being "a starkly challenging and slightly repulsive picture of biblical thinking . . . true to neo-orthodox thinking, if not to biblical realities."[16] In a review for the *Journal for the Scientific Study of Religion*, sociologist Jeffrey Hadden—himself author of the influential book *Metropolis in Crisis: Social and Political Perspectives*—characterized Ellul's work as a simple recitation of the anti-urban sentiments of the biblical authors.[17] In statements characteristic of the wider reception of the book, both reviewers suggested that Ellul's approach justified at best "benign neglect" of lost and cursed cities by Christians preoccupied with the eschatological city. If, as Ellul argued, God would put all things right in the end, and if in the meantime we could not fix things ourselves, then why involve ourselves in the city at all? Both Winter and Hadden believed Ellul to be excusing Christians from involvement in shaping the course of history and, specifically, from shaping the fate of the city. By supposedly proof-texting anti-urban sentiments in Scripture, Ellul was giving Christians an excuse to despise the city themselves.

To this date, the majority sentiment among urbanists seems to be that *The Meaning of the City* should have been titled, *Demeaning the City*. But did the one-time Deputy Mayor of Bordeaux really advocate leaving a lost and cursed city to rot, waiting quietly for the final work of the new creation? Or have commentators misinterpreted Ellul? Indeed, *The Meaning of the City* may be one of Ellul's most misunderstood works, owing largely to the fact that it occupies a distinctive place in Ellul's corpus as an ambitious argument that attempts to offer theologically based hope in response to despairing inquiries by social theorists.

Revelation and Reason in The Meaning of the City

While *The Meaning of the City* was written in the language of international urbanism, it was not written on the terms of international urbanism. That is, rather than take for granted the questions and methods of urbanism, *The Meaning of the City* was first and foremost a critique of those very questions and methods. When Ellul waded into this debate, it was not to say, "You've

---

16. Winter, review of *Meaning of the City*, 118.
17. Hadden, "Is God a Country Boy?"

The City and Urbanism

got your questions and methods pretty much right, but you need to tweak some things at the margins." Rather, it was to say that urbanism itself fails to deal effectively and powerfully with the reality of the city and, therefore, to understand fully the presence and influence of the city in the world.

For Ellul, in order to understand the city, we should let Scripture set the agenda. We should allow the Christian faith to interrogate and critique urbanism rather than conform ourselves to the urbanist's way of thinking. Only then might we rightly understand what urbanism and the other "sciences" teach us about the city. Only then will we be able to act in true service to our increasingly urban society. Here it is worth quoting Ellul at great length:

> Have the Scriptures perchance taught us something decisive concerning the concrete situation in which we find ourselves? If so, all of the historical and sociological problems take a subordinate role.
>
> For if the word of God is truly marked out for us in the Scriptures and if it is truly spoken for us, taking hold of us in our concrete situation, and if at the same time as it takes hold of us (for our condemnation and salvation) it enlightens our understanding of that situation, and if we are truly involved in the city and the Bible shows us where we are in the city and what the city means for us and our relations with her, then all that we have learned should form the proper nucleus of a science of the city. Not of an objective and purely technical science of the city, but a science in which we would be involved as in a struggle for the truth. For the basic question is whether we can deal with a foreign and unalterable truth, whether we can conquer and possess it, or whether by launching into such a quest we become involved in it ourselves and responsible for it, responsible for what we will learn and what we will do with this truth. And since man knows no science but a concrete science, then by studying the city are we not working for a human science?
>
> And since man knows no science but a science built up according to a plan, then by seeking the spiritual nucleus of this problem are we not working for a human science? What is striking in modern research is that it just happens not to be built up around a plan; it is guided by the objects under study, follows every whim of its instruments, and is constantly led on by the successive discovery of new objects for study. It imposes no domination, and while it is praiseworthy in its humility, it is also vain in its incoherency. We do not believe that such an approach is necessary any more than is the idol of objectivity. And when we have revealed, as here, the spiritual nucleus of a problem, we admit (and this is also singularly

> humble) that it is in fact the nucleus of the problem, that every aspect radiates around it. If we accept this, then what we learn to know about the city by natural means, by history and sociology, and about man in the city by psychology and the novel, must be connected, coordinated, strongly knotted together, because of the spiritual nucleus. The result is that our natural sources are dependent on revelation. I know that this will be considered a betrayal to science, but it is either this method or else the sterility of death. How is it that our historians and sociologists have not been struck with the sterility of their work? Our work of tying the threads together will not be done explicitly, for we have already traced their pattern. Our entire purpose will be to come to a decision and to take our biblical information to its logical conclusions.[18]

Note that the "human sciences" are not at all absent from Ellul's account. While they are subordinated to biblical and theological inquiry—and for this Ellul expects to be regarded as a traitor to progress—they play an important role. While alone they are insufficient, properly subordinated to Scripture they help us to "act in true service to society." For Ellul, God's revelation, his supernatural act of making himself known, serves to organize, interpret, and empower the data gathered by natural means. Again, Ellul:

> Certitude can be found only in the position that revelation forces us to adopt with regard to the spiritual being of the city and its role through history as concerns man. The reality of the city, not as an event, but as a structure of the world, can be understood only in the light of revelation. And this revelation provides us with both a means of understanding the problem and a synthesis of its aspects as found in the raw data of history and sociology. However, we must not expect perfect agreement, for the two realities are not on the same plane. Although I cannot mistake the sun for the colors of the spectrum, nevertheless, I could not know color but by the help of the sun. I could doubtlessly make a chemical analysis of the coloring agents, I could study all the physical or biological aspects of color, without ever having an inkling of living color, unless all these aspects are brought into play by the simple fact of light bringing out color.
>
> So it is with the reality of human problems in general and with our particular aspect of life. Revelation—which was not given with this in mind—enlightens, brings together, and explains what our reason and experience discover. Without revelation, all our reasoning is doubtlessly useful, but does not view reality in true

---

18. Ellul, *Meaning of the City*, 147–48.

perspective. So when we said that we had nothing new to offer history or sociology, we were correct, but not strictly. We have in fact furnished no direct contribution to these sciences themselves; but what history and sociology tell us about the city is here confronted with revelation, is brought together and synthesized not as bare fact but as illuminated by another source of light.[19]

Of all of Ellul's books, *The Meaning of the City* contains some of the most explicit statements of his agenda for relating faith and reason, supernatural revelation and the natural and social sciences. Ellul allowed revelation to give order to what was learned through reason. This meta-methodological issue is what lends the book to misunderstanding. It is not only an approach that is foreign to secular urbanism, but it jeopardizes the primacy of urbanism's questions and methods and offends many by its implicit exclusivity. These issues blind some readers even to what Ellul seems to say so very clearly, including his admission of the majesty of the city and human responsibility toward its social challenges.

So what, in fact, did Ellul find when he brought scriptural resources to bear upon the interpretation and organization of what the human sciences say about the city? Ellul's investigation into the Scriptures led him to the conclusion that the city is the greatest achievement of human beings and the center of all other cultural achievements. According to Ellul, the arts flourish in the city. Government and law are developed in the city. Educational and other institutions are not only common to the city, but depend upon it for their development.

At this point, one might wonder exactly what urbanists and others have found so offensive about Ellul's argument. The city is the greatest achievement of human beings and the key to all other accomplishments. What's not to like? How is Ellul demeaning the city?

Ellul's Approach to the Biblical Witness Regarding the City

Ellul's approach to Scripture is more or less organized around the categories of creation, redemption, and consummation. According to this rubric, he investigates the "reality of the city" as presented by the biblical data. His inquiry answers, either explicitly or implicitly, the following questions: What does Scripture attest regarding the city as part of God's good creation? What does Scripture attest regarding the city after the fall and the curse,

19. Ibid., 153–54.

as a part of the created order in need of redemption? What does Scripture attest regarding the consummation of God's plans for the city, regarding the city in the new creation?

The City in Need of Redemption

Readers familiar with the biblical narrative will immediately see one of the challenges of this approach: There is no account of a city preceding the fall of humanity into sin and subsequent curse announced in Genesis 3. Unlike many other topics—say, for example, the human mind, sexuality, flora and fauna—one cannot straightforwardly locate and describe what the biblical data have to say about the city and creation. One is left to speculate about the relationship between what we can know about the reality of the city and what we know about prototypical human community before the fall. To consider the city and creation, one strategy might be to investigate the city as one expression of human sociality, which originates in the social order described by Genesis 1 and 2 and affirmed by God as "very good." In other words, one might recognize the city as one expression of human community and begin an investigation into its spiritual reality as described in Scripture by locating Scripture's first testimonies about human community before the fall and curse.

Ellul, however, does not begin by recognizing the city as one expression of human community and relating it to the prototypical social order described in Genesis 1 and 2. For Ellul, the story of the city begins after the account of the fall and the curse with Gen 4:1–17: the story of Cain. Most people—even nonreligious people—are familiar with the beginning of the story. Following their expulsion from the Garden of Eden, Adam and Eve had two children, Cain and Abel. The brothers presented sacrifices to God: Abel brought a sheep, the firstborn of his flock, which pleased God, while Cain brought part of his harvest, which displeased God. Angry and envious, Cain killed his brother. God called Cain to account for his brother's whereabouts: "Where is your brother Abel?" (Gen 4:9). Infamously, Cain replied that he did not know and asked, "Am I my brother's keeper?" (Gen 4:9). Even though Cain was not forthcoming, God knew what Cain had done and, as a punishment for Cain's deeds, cursed him: "What have you done? Listen! The voice of your brother's blood cries out to me from the ground. Now you are under a curse and driven from the ground, which opened its mouth to receive your brother's blood from your hand. When you work the ground, it will no longer yield its crops for you. You will be a restless wanderer on the earth" (Gen 4:10–12). Cain protested: "My punishment is greater than I can bear. Today you are driving me from the land, and I will be hidden from your presence; I will be a restless wanderer on the earth, and whoever finds me will kill me" (Gen 4:13–14). Cain feared the wandering life, the insecurity of alienation not only from the land and from God, but also from human community, which he shattered through violence. Mercifully, God put a mark on Cain that was meant to protect him on his journey, to provide him with the security he would need to endure his discipline with obedience. After wandering to the east, Cain settled in the land of Nod and built a city named after his son, Enoch (Gen 4:16–17).

For Ellul, this first scriptural reference to a city communicates the "spiritual reality" of all cities. "If this story is significant," he writes, ". . . it is because it gives us God's view of man, or rather God's view of certain attitudes and activities of man."[20] According to Ellul, the shape of this story suggests that construction of the first city was an act of rebellion against God. Until Cain murdered Abel, God's grace "enabled life to go on, and this protection is seen in a certain stability, a certain familiarity between man and nature. He has introduced insecurity, the taste for blood, for vengeance. And the condemnation pronounced by God is only the inevitable result of Cain's act. Cain has broken the relationship between man and the world, and so he will necessarily be a fugitive and a wanderer."[21] After his crime and curse, Cain had neither a home nor the security a home provides. Though he received assurance through a sign of God's protection, "he would prefer a more obvious security, such as the one he destroyed by his crime—family security, a relationship with animals and things, a familiarity with men and places."[22] So Cain builds a city. As Ellul writes,

> Cain is completely dissatisfied with the security granted to him by God, and so he searches out his own security. . . . As for his security, he will find another way to procure it. . . . He will take care of his own needs in these areas . . . The city for Cain is first of all the place where he can be himself—his homeland, the one settled spot in his wandering. Secondly, it is a material sign of his security. He is responsible for himself and for his life. He is far from the Lord's face, and so he will shift for himself. Cain sought security not so

---

20. Ellul, *Meaning of the City*, 2.
21. Ibid.
22. Ibid.

> much from God, whom he was trying to escape, as from the world, hostile since Abel's murder. The world was perhaps difficult after Adam's fall, but it was not yet marked by murder. Now it is. The city is the direct consequence of Cain's murderous act and of his refusal to accept God's protection.
>
> Cain has built a city. For God's Eden he substitutes his own, for the goal given to his life by God, he substitutes a goal chosen by himself—just as he substituted his own security for God's. Such is the act by which Cain takes his destiny on his own shoulders, refusing the hand of God in his life.[23]

Enoch the city was a product of Cain's refusal to accept his discipline with obedience and to be a wanderer on the earth. Moreover, it was a product of Cain's refusal to trust in the promises of a God who had given his special mark of protection. Cain should have wandered as God directed, trusting God's mark to preserve him in the face of death. Instead, he built a city in order to regain a sense of security conferred by stability and community, rather than by faith.

Ellul believed that the spiritual reality of every city was determined by Enoch's founding as a rejection of God's promise in favor of self-realization and self-expression. A rejection of spiritual promises of security and prosperity in favor of material signs of security and prosperity would characterize all cities from then on. Babel, Babylon, Nineveh, Sodom and Gomorrah: it is no wonder that these cities would be known for their rebellion. The apples didn't fall far from the tree.

The City and New Creation

So much for what Scripture teaches us about the city after the fall and the curse—about the city in need of redemption. It is easier now to see why Ellul's detractors believed that he maligned the city. Sure, he believed it was the most significant human achievement—even the *sine qua non* of a host of other achievements—but he believed that this achievement represented a fundamental rejection of God and God's promises. Self-expression and self-realization, for Ellul, are expressions of our sinfulness, even when they issue in great achievements.

If this were as far as Ellul went, his urbanist critics might be justified. But Ellul's analysis does not end with what Scripture attests regarding the

---

23. Ibid., 4–5.

city after the fall. Ellul continues to consider what Scripture attests concerning the intersection of the city and eschatological hope. His analysis in this vein begins with Jerusalem and ends with the new Jerusalem. Ellul writes of Jerusalem: "Jerusalem is a holy city. But she is still a city. She carries man's mark, even in her election, even in her adoption by God. She never escapes from all the characteristics of the city, as is indicated by the accusations constantly aimed at her, aimed at the sins she never ceases falling into anew. Her sins are those of other cities; she acts like them and is condemned like them."[24] Jerusalem is a bloody and idolatrous city, and yet one covered by God's unfailing love and chosen for his special purposes.[25] As Timothy Gorringe notes, this tension is central to Ellul's argument concerning the city and does resemble in some ways the dialectic of urbanists such as Lewis Mumford and David Harvey.[26]

Jerusalem represents the "already and not yet" of the city in the promised new creation. According to Ellul, Jerusalem is consecrated unto God, and "everything in the city of Jerusalem that still belongs to the world of the city, the creation and pride of man, is condemned to be only a devastated cemetery."[27] God does not give to Jerusalem a perfect politics and a righteous army. The remnants of the old city remain. But God is present in this city, among these remnants, opening up new possibilities. God's presence in Jerusalem is a sign of both his adoption and his judgment. And it is a sign, Ellul writes, "to all the cities of the world."[28] In his promise to make Jerusalem great by making it his, through both his condemnation and adoption, God promises to overcome the spiritual reality of the city: because of God's promise to transform the city, *all cities* "are recipients of a marvelous destiny in Jesus Christ."[29] And it is through the work of Jesus Christ that God's promise for the city is fulfilled.

The work of Jesus Christ represents both martyrdom and miracle. His suffering and death represent spectacular failure, while his resurrection and ascension promise spectacular success. Because God incarnate is condemned and killed in Jerusalem, it fulfills man's purposes for the city as a place of human self-expression, self-sufficiency, and self-realization and

24. Ellul, *Meaning of the City*, 97.
25. Ibid., 97–100.
26. Gorringe, *Theology of the Built Environment*, l1925.
27. Ellul, *Meaning of the City*, 101.
28. Ibid., 105.
29. Ibid., 140.

stands under God's judgment. At the same time, the resurrection of the king of the Jews, a king from David's line who would sit forever on a throne in Jerusalem, requires redemption of the city. It demands consummation of God's promises to the city, his promise to dwell in it forever, no longer spiting the fact that it is a sign of rebellion against him, but transforming its spiritual reality. This eschatological consummation will be realized in the new Jerusalem, the heavenly city of the Revelation of John.

Ethical Implications

The new Jerusalem is coming. God will redeem the city when he consummates the new creation brought about by the work of his Word, Jesus Christ. This redemption is most certainly not a work of urban planners and policymakers working according to natural means. Ellul believed that natural means to urban revitalization would be futile, that the city awaited a supernatural and eschatological intervention.

But what are Christians to do in the meantime? How are they to behave in and toward cities that are still the creation and pride of man and yet are redeemed by the work of Jesus Christ? If the city stands under God's judgment, should Christians abandon it? If God has already accomplished his redemption of the city, and we only await its consummation, should Christians do nothing? The keys to understanding what Ellul believes we must do are the rubric of "miracle and martyrdom" and the contrast between "faithfulness and success."

Miracle and Martyrdom

For Ellul, Christians are called to the city in imitation of the ministry of Jesus Christ, whose work in Jerusalem represented both martyrdom and miracle. Christians are without question called to live and work in the city. In doing so, they represent the presence of God in the midst of the self-assertion, self-realization, and self-sufficiency of human beings—the body of Christ, as God's greatest accomplishment, in the midst of the greatest accomplishment of his rebellious creatures. Our presence in the city should signify and symbolize what the heavenly city of God will be like and that it will be different from the city of man. For this betrayal of the city and the self-sufficiency that it symbolizes, Christians should expect rejection and suffering. In other words, they should expect to follow Jesus' footsteps into martyrdom.

If the city does not reject us, then this is, strictly speaking, miraculous. Like the resurrection and ascension, this is a *super*natural event that requires God's intervention. For people of faith in a God who performs miracles and rules over nature, this is perfectly conceivable, even if it is both unexpected and unlikely. For this reason, Christians should not prejudge whether our faithful representation of God's judgment upon and adoption of the city, of the promised triumph of faith over self-assertion, self-realization, and self-sufficiency, will result in miracle or martyrdom. That is up to God. We know we are called to the city. We cannot know whether our calling is to martyrdom or to miracle.

Faithfulness versus Success

A corollary of Ellul's miracle/martyrdom rubric is the importance of faithfulness. For Ellul, Christians are called to faithfulness rather than to success. The task of the church is not to bring in the kingdom of God. As Ellul notes elsewhere, the kingdom of God marches toward us; we do not march toward it.[30] While we await the coming kingdom, our task is to faithfully symbolize and signify what the kingdom of God is like. We do this in the city in order to serve as signs of God's love: "Not only do God's people in the midst of the city already serve as God's presence, but much more important, they serve also as the temporal election of the city itself, to accomplish God's work . . . and the promise made to the city. All this is to show that the condemnation of the city has not plunged her into morningless night."[31] Faithfulness is to face the uncertainty of miracle or martyrdom with courage and hope, signifying these truths of God's love for the city and his work, even if it appears that the city will not accept that testimony.

An overarching commitment to success compromises faithfulness. Such a prejudice is itself a commitment to the same sort of self-assertion, self-realization, and self-sufficiency that are at the heart of human rebellion against God. It involves the presumption that we know perfectly what ought to be, that we should bring about those conditions no matter the cost. A commitment to faithfulness, on the other hand, is a commitment to symbolize and signify what the kingdom of God is like, whether or not it seems successful, even if it might lead to martyrdom. Faithfulness takes "failure" seriously as an option.

30. Ellul, "Christian Faith and Social Reality," 174, 179.
31. Ellul, *Meaning of the City*, 90.

An overarching commitment to faithfulness rather than to success ensures that the people of God witness to his work in both success and failure, both miracle and martyrdom. Miraculous successes of Christian involvement in the city signify what the kingdom of God is like. If the people of God are faithful despite suffering and hardship, then spectacular failure and martyrdom testify that, unlike Cain, we will trust God and hope in his promised new creation rather than assert our self-sufficiency.

The Paradox of Ellulian Urbanism: Apocalyptic and Prophetic Urbanism

It is clear that many of Ellul's detractors were confused or unfair in their assertion that Ellul was excusing Christians from involvement in the city. No doubt this owes at least in part to Ellul's seemingly thoroughgoing rejection of human interventions that might improve urban life. In *The Meaning of the City*, Ellul not only asserted that supernatural intervention was necessary for the redemption of the city, but he asserted that natural means to urban revitalization would be futile. In response to plans such as Le Corbusier's idea to "create great blocks of dwellings where people will meet one another as they did in the village, with everything (grocer, baker, butcher) included in the block so that people will get to know each other and a community will come into being," Ellul wrote, "The result of Le Corbusier's creation was exactly the opposite of what had been planned; problems of loneliness and isolation in such blocks of dwellings proved to be much more tragic than in the normal and traditional city."[32] Ellul's argument in *The Meaning of the City* appears to leave no room for the possibility that interventions in social institutions or the physical environment might bring about any significant change. In this way, he seems to marginalize the interventions of urban planners and others. Some readers interpret this as a rejection of the potential for interventions in social institutions and the physical environment to bring about important and positive moral formation. Yet even Ellul's response to Le Corbusier suggests the possibility for such interventions to make a positive contribution to human flourishing—the "normal and traditional city" is better, according to Ellul, than Le Corbusier's machines for living.

What Ellul chiefly intends is that no human intervention can change the *spiritual reality* of the city. Indeed, Ellul writes, "There would be no reason for optimism even if the projects of the urbanists were launched and

32. Ellul, *Technological Society*, 420.

Le Corbusier's 'House of Mankind' were built. In very little time, the city would become herself again. No change in the walls, no purification of the air or improvement in lighting, no mixture of greenery and cement could transform the city's spiritual being."[33] Ellul was no more sanguine about the humanist and modernist impulses at the heart of city planning:

> How ridiculous, how grotesque is bravado of naked little man—bravado filling every newspaper, every socialist doctrine, every Protestant journal, every belief in the rebirth of humanism. "I am, and there is none else," man shouts. "I will stop the whole mess, I will put it in order. It's not so bad as it seems. This [urban distress] is only the normal course of history, a change of civilizations. There is no reason to be afraid of these new developments. In a few decades we will be familiar with them. All we have to do is to adapt and not reject them . . . and we must expand our minds in order to dominate them. We'll handle it."[34] Poor little man. You failed to notice that you are not dealing with flesh and blood, but with Thrones, and Powers, and Dominations which are attacking you, grinding you under, dominating you from every side, and that the Devil's last trick is to make you think that you can put order back into chaos, that you are going to get spiritually big enough to the control the world.[35]

In condemning the spiritual meaning of the city, Ellul appears to marginalize practical interventions in urban life and to overlook the possibility that interventions can make an important difference. He appears to overlook the possibility for good urban planning and policy to promote freedom and justice, for the built environment to "promote human virtue or destroy it."[36]

Readers should note, however, that this reflects Ellul's tendency, in *The Meaning of the City*, toward the "apocalyptic" over the "prophetic," which leads him to emphasize what is common between human enterprises and how they differ from the kingdom of God and to marginalize the differences between human enterprises.[37] In an effort to undermine *all* sources of

33. Ibid., 158.

34. This quote not only reflects the spirit of urbanism in Ellul's day, but specifically mimics a passage from Lewis Mumford's *City in History*.

35. Ellul, *Meaning of the City*, 166.

36. Gorringe, *Theology of the Built Environment*, 157.

37. It is important to note that *The Meaning of the City* is not the only work in which the city plays a role in emphasizing the infinite distance of human enterprises from the kingdom of God. In *Apocalypse*, Ellul's commentary on the book of Revelation, Ellul focuses on the biblical text's juxtaposition of the new Jerusalem and Babylon.

false hope,[38] Ellul appears to elide truly important differences between ways of organizing human community. While Ellul is pronouncing "the *non possumus*" against "renewed passion for the city," condemning the spiritual meaning of the city, he presses practical interventions to the margins and *appears* to overlook the possibility that interventions can make an important difference.

Yet this tendency belies a contravening tendency in the rest of Ellul's work or life. In other works, he clearly shows negative moral and ecological impacts of developments in social institutions and the physical environment. For example, if in *The Technological Society* some developments in human institutions and the built environment can stunt freedom and justice and undermine human virtue, then other developments would, in fact, be better for everyone. It is also important to note Ellul's activism, public service in municipal government, and engagement with secular academia, all of which point to the promise of engagement and the differences between interventions in the built environment and social institutions. Indeed, Ellul argues that Christians should be actively engaged in urban planning, policy, and design, even while they should not be "building the city" in a spiritual sense. And accounting for many of Ellul's other contributions to the intersection of Christian life and social ethics, it is evident that Ellul does see important differences between human endeavors, which opens up the possibility of interpreting Ellul "prophetically" and not just "apocalyptically." While this "prophetic" position may have been overshadowed by Ellul's "apocalyptic" proclivities in *The Meaning of the City*, it is clearly evident when we take the wider view.

Ellul's Contribution and Continuing Importance

Timothy Gorringe—whose interpretation of Ellul's arguments and sentiments concerning the city ring truest to our own assessment—writes that Ellul was the "leading Reformed commentator on the city in the twentieth

---

38. In his commentary on Ecclesiastes, Ellul sums up Qohelet's message with the following quote from George Bernano: "In order to be prepared to hope in what does not deceive, we must first lose hope in *everything* that deceives" (Ellul, *Reason for Being*, 47). Keith L. Johnson has discerned this impulse in Ellul, citing *The Meaning of the City* in his chapter on sin and depravity in the hit television show *The Wire*, which is set in inner-city Baltimore. In his work, Johnson points out that *The Wire*'s pessimistic posture toward all social institutions is consistent with a commitment to hope only in the one who does not deceive. See Johnson, "Depravity and Hope in the City."

century."[39] This alone would make Ellul an important figure for understanding urbanization and urbanism. It is also true, though, that many of Ellul's insights into the city are as important today as they were in 1970. Sometime between 2005 and 2008, global population passed a watershed mark. For the first time in history, more than 50 percent of the world's population lived in cities. The impact of this demographic shift is likely, according to some scholars, to be as significant as when people first started to live in cities in large numbers.[40] Human settlement in larger and increasingly dense cities will have profound impacts upon diversity, identity, citizenship, culture, environment, and governance. Some cities are now regarded as "cosmopoli": cities in which the whole world is represented. The diversity of such cities has important impacts upon notions of identity and citizenship, who we think we are and to whom we have obligations. Shifting senses of identity and citizenship in increasingly diverse cities can result in cooperative pursuit of the common good or radicalization. What happens in large cities is also important to the shape of the global environment. For example, cities like Shanghai actually affect the quality of the environment on the West Coast of the United States, demonstrating their global reach. This global reach extends to matters of governance, as cities are increasingly influential as sites and actors in global politics. Therefore, we live in an increasingly urban world—one in which the meaning of the city is an increasingly important matter for discernment and *The Meaning of the City* remains an important guide to that discernment. Ellul's work on technique and the city is relevant today to the approaches taken to novel urban forms, such as megalopolises and megaslums.[41] Ellul's specific focus on the presence and influence of the city in the world, if not his focus on the city's spiritual meaning, is now widely echoed in the burgeoning literature on cities.

In 1970, Ellul wrote, "Whatever direction we envisage for the future of our civilization, it is only too correct to think of it as *the triumph of the city*."[42] In his 2011 book *Triumph of the City: How Our Greatest Invention Makes Us Richer, Smarter, Greener, Healthier, and Happier*, Harvard economist Edward Glaeser argues that cities, "our species' greatest invention," have

---

39. Gorringe, *Theology of the Built Environment*, l१591.

40. McNeill, "Cities and Their Consequences."

41. See Wang, "Ellul on New Urbanism," for a treatment of one particular mode of city planning from an Ellulian perspective.

42. Ellul, *Meaning of the City*, 158.

"triumphed."[43] Demographic, political, economic, and cultural transitions currently underway all demonstrate a dramatic shift of our social center of gravity toward the urban. Glaeser expects a future "emerald green age of the city" in which the efficiencies of urban settlement make social and environmental challenges easier to confront in effective fashion.[44] The city is and will be, according to Glaeser, the source of the goods we hold to be most precious: "whether in London's ornate arcades or Rio's fractious favelas, whether in the high-rises of Hong Kong or the dusty workspaces of Dharavis, our culture, our prosperity, and our freedom are all ultimately gifts of people living, working, and thinking together—the ultimate triumph of the city."[45]

For Glaeser, this triumph comes in the face of significant social and environmental challenges that attend to urban agglomerations all over the world. Despite these challenges and problems, the city provides us with unprecedented security, prosperity, and sustainability. This is a theme that pervades other texts as well. David Owen argues in *Green Metropolis* that, because people in cities have lower levels of environmental impact—they live smaller, live closer together, and drive less—cities are the solution to global environmental challenges.[46] Cities are also key drivers of an increasingly global economy because they provide access to the world through infrastructure for global air travel, making them machines for competition and economic growth.[47] More and more people are dependent upon increasingly influential cities for their security and prosperity. Ellul confronts us with questions about the sources and signs of our security and prosperity in the face of difficult challenges to our increasingly urban world. Will we, like Cain, spend ourselves "trying to find security, struggling against hostile forces, dominating men and nature, taking guarantees that are within his reach, guarantees that *appear* to him to be genuine, but which in fact protect him from nothing"?[48] What will be our response to the soteriological mythology of the city—the idea that through the city itself we will find our salvation? What does it mean to engage with the city in such a way as testifies to the work of God to redeem the city? Ellul's approach to cities—allowing the biblical narrative to set the agenda—also remains important

43. Glaeser, *Triumph of the City*.
44. Ibid..
45. Ibid..
46. Owen, *Green Metropolis*.
47. Kasarda and Lindsay, *Aerotropolis*.
48. Ellul, *Meaning of the City*, 3.

both for the necessary prophetic urbanism in a world of megaslums and for the necessary apocalyptic element in a world that tempts us to believe that global urbanity itself can deliver us from evil.

Far from the sort of science to which Mumford and others had devoted themselves, Ellul's approach actually undermined many of their most important assumptions. This was the most important contribution that Ellul made to urbanism. Reading Ellul required reckoning with an approach that was entirely foreign, one that challenged and interrogated predominant approaches to studying the city. For this, Ellul was regarded as a fool, and perhaps with good reason. In his novel *Foucault's Pendulum*, Umberto Eco's protagonists discuss the nature of foolishness:

> "Being a fool is . . . complicated. It's a form of social behavior. A fool is one who always talks outside his glass."
>
> "What do you mean?"
>
> "Like this." He pointed at the counter near his glass. "He wants to talk about what's in the glass, but somehow or other he misses. He's the guy who puts his foot in his mouth. For example, he says how's your lovely wife to someone whose wife has just left him."
>
> "Yes, I know a few of those."
>
> "Fools are in great demand, especially on social occasions. They embarrass everyone, but provide material for conversation. In their positive form, they become diplomats. Talking outside the glass when someone else blunders helps to change the subject. But fools don't interest us, either. They're never creative, their talent is all second-hand, so they don't submit manuscripts to publishers. Fools don't claim that cats bark, but they talk about cats when everyone else is talking about dogs. They offend all the rules of conversation . . ."

Just when most other public intellectuals were preoccupied with social-scientific appraisals of the city and its challenges, Ellul offered a biblical-theological appraisal of the spiritual reality at the root of its many issues. He didn't claim that revelation could answer the same questions as the natural sciences—he didn't claim that cats bark. Rather, he claimed that revelation provided the questions and answers that ought to organize our inquiry into cities—he talked about cats when everyone else was talking about dogs. He offended all the rules of conversation.

In this way, Ellul's work was an example of privileging faithfulness rather than success. Ellul did not presume to know whether his testimony would miraculously be accepted or would end in spectacular failure, rejection, and martyrdom. Nevertheless, his work is a witness to dependence upon the supernatural revelation of God, rather than a self-sufficient reliance upon the natural and social sciences alone, to ask and answer the right questions about the city. This is the most important contribution that Ellul made through *The Meaning of the City*, and it applies not only to urbanism but to other inquiries as well.

CHAPTER 5

Politics and Economics

"It seems important to me that in all parties (including even in the communist party) there should be Christians and that the role of these Christians should be to be well in tune with and serious comrades for those who are in the same party, but that they unceasingly remember, and that is the significance of their political commitment, that they are more united with their brothers in Jesus Christ who belong to the opposite party than with their comrades of the same party."[1]

ELLUL LIVED AND WROTE during a time of conflict and great political upheaval. He lived his early childhood in the shadow of World War I. By the time he gained his first faculty position, the world was in the throes of its second great war of the century. World War II, during which Ellul's home country, France, was occupied by the armies of Nazi Germany and then liberated by the Allied military, pitted the forces of fascism against those of democracy and socialism. During the war, Ellul served the French resistance to Nazi occupation, though he never took up arms. As noted in chapter 1, for assisting Jews in their flight from Nazi persecution, he was eventually awarded the status of "Righteous Among the Nations" by Yad Vashem in Jerusalem, the Holocaust Martyrs' and Heroes' Remembrance Authority.

The time of Ellul's greatest scholarly contributions was marked by the Cold War. From VJ-Day until just before Ellul's death in 1994, the world witnessed continual low-intensity conflict, high-risk deployments of

---

1. Ellul, "Christian Faith and Social Reality," 179.

nuclear weapons, and a battle for the hearts and minds of the world—a battle eventually won by democratic capitalism in no small part because the Communist bloc spent its way into oblivion trying to outproduce the capitalist world.

During the Cold War, countries devoted to democratic capitalism worked against those devoted to socialism in order to persuade or force countries of the so-called Third World to join their cause. Investments in propaganda and the propagation of conflict were extreme. Proxy wars were fought in newly decolonized parts of Africa, Asia, and Latin America. Loyalties were tested and retested. The "middle ground" was most often occupied only by the most wretched—the poor, who felt despised by both sides. In this environment, one would think that Ellul, as a public intellectual, would weigh in on one side or the other. To do so was a popular activity among public intellectuals, as were high-profile defections from one side to the other. A scholar who had worked in the history of law and social institutions would have been expected to hold an opinion.

As has been noted in chapter 1, Ellul was, for a time, a devotee of Karl Marx (1818–1883), whose work Ellul had discovered at the age of eighteen.[2] Marx, a German philosopher, sociologist, and economic historian, was the fountainhead of the socialist movement. Marx was a historical materialist—he believed patterns of production, distribution, and consumption of material goods determined ideas and drove social change. Moreover, he thought that all social systems included inherent tensions that would eventually result in crises leading to the replacement of one social system by another. For example, he insisted that class tensions would lead to a crisis in capitalism, which would be replaced by socialism, which would in turn be replaced by communism. Marx advocated a socialist revolution, led by the poor and working class, in order to bring about the shift away from capitalism. Marx's two greatest theoretical contributions were *The Communist Manifesto* and *Capital*, in which he offered what appeared to some to be a devastating critique of capitalism and its vices.[3]

Ellul had found in Marx someone with wide-ranging capacities for comprehensive social critique—someone who had taken seriously the study of human institutions in the unfolding of history. In an interview,

---

2. Ellul, "New Karl Marx," 29.

3. Marx and Engels, *Communist Manifesto*; Marx, *Capital* (3 vols.). See also Marx, *Grundrisse*. For a brief introduction to *Capital*, see Harvey, *Companion to Marx's Capital*. For a very short introduction to Marx, see Singer, *Marx*.

he indicated that Marx's comprehensiveness was the source of his appeal: "I discovered a global interpretation of the world, the explanation for this drama of misery and decadence that we [as a family] had experienced. The excellence of Marx's thinking, in the domain of economic theory, convinced me. . . . [I]t was the first breakthrough giving me a general interpretation of the world, my first general education."[4] Ellul was captivated by Marx's far-reaching, bold, and incisive analysis and claimed to have read and annotated all of Marx's writings.[5]

After Ellul became a Christian, though, he rejected Marx*ism*. He found its political agenda, calls for violent revolution, rejection of religion, and lack of attention to human agency offensive. But *he did not reject the critical agenda of Marx*—his attempt to offer a comprehensive critique of the predominant social order. Nor did he reject the dialectical approach that was characteristic of Marx, which Marx himself picked up from Hegel and which laid some of the groundwork for Ellul's attraction to Barth. Ellul explained his persistent affinity for Marxist analysis despite his rejection of Marxist ideology, saying he broke with

> the kind of Marxism that claims to be the aim of and the key to everything. On the other hand, I totally agree with a Marxism that offers a method of interpretation. I also agree with a Marxism that provides some opportunity for political action. All the while, I recognize the dangers of Marxism that were already present in Marx's writing. Marxism as a sociological study of capitalism does not imply any belief. Belief comes into play, first, when Marxism takes on a messianic, revolutionary dimension . . . and second when it is considered a science in every domain. In reality, it is pure belief to call Marxism a science. This belief is always dangerous. I can no longer truly believe that Marxism represents the ultimate in science, the ultimate in truth. In these areas, I would say that, on the contrary, when Marxism becomes dogmatic it is actually a lie.[6]

In fact, despite his reservations about the prescriptive political economic dimensions of Marx's analysis, Ellul declared that we needed more social theorists with the power, acumen, and scope that Marx demonstrated in his analysis of capitalism. In his essay "Needed: A New Karl Marx!" he asserted that the reach of technological society and its afflictions would

---

4. Garrigou-Lagrange, *In Season*, 11.
5. Ellul, *Ellul on Religion, Technology, and Politics*, 87.
6. Ibid., 60–61.

demand equally grand critique. Understanding the twentieth century would require someone with insight as comprehensive and powerful as that of Marx.[7]

Ellul himself brought this kind of comprehensive and powerful insight to his critique of political economic systems. Because of what Ellul found so penetrating and admirable about Marx's critique, he set a similarly ambitious agenda for his own work in political economy. This resulted in a more or less "one size fits all" assessment of fascism, socialism, and capitalism alike. While some would emphasize gulfs between these systems, Ellul remarked on subtle differences while emphasizing great similarities. This is in part attributable to his preoccupations with totalitarianism and technique, against which he leveled a critique so grand as to *encompass* all of the main political economic systems of his time. So while Ellul did offer an opinion, he did not exactly take sides. He was an equal opportunity critic. Ellul took to task capitalism, communism, fascism, as well as money, work, and the state, in ways informed by social theory, biblical studies, and theology.

Political Economic Systems Common during Ellul's Life

One of the most striking aspects of Ellul's positions on political economy is his consistent use of the concepts of technique and totalitarianism across different political economic systems. This accounts for the fact that Ellul's analyses of various political economic systems can seem very similar. He can levy the same charges against fascism, capitalism, and socialism. This does not mean, however, that he saw all three of these systems in the same way, that he believed they were uniform. On the contrary, he understood well the differences between them, but he saw that all three were pursuing similar goals according to different means *and* that the use of different means was simply a technical question. That is, the three differed primarily in their selections of the "one best way" to achieve their common goals of facilitating the accumulation of money and power. While their approaches differed, it is important to note that, from Ellul's perspective, they were engaged in an ongoing debate not concerning the ends of social life, but concerning the means by which those ends would be best secured.

---

7. Ellul, "New Karl Marx."

Fascism

Fascism is the "totalitarian philosophy of government that glorifies the state and nation and assigns to the state control over every aspect of national life."[8] The term is generally used as "a generic name for a particular brand of totalitarian regime, several of which made their appearance in Europe between 1922 and 1936."[9] Historians typically emphasize three characteristics of fascism:[10]

- First and most important is the glorification of the state and the total subordination of the individual to it. The state is defined as an organic whole into which individuals must be absorbed for their own and the state's benefit. This "total state" is absolute in its methods and unlimited by law in its control and direction of its citizens.

- A second ruling concept of fascism is embodied in the theory of social Darwinism. The doctrine of survival of the fittest and the necessity of struggle for life is applied by fascists to the life of a nation-state. Peaceful, complacent nations are seen as doomed to fall before more dynamic ones, making struggle and aggressive militarism a leading characteristic of the fascist state. Imperialism is the logical outcome of this dogma.

- Another element of fascism is its elitism. Salvation from rule by the mob and the destruction of the existing social order can be effected only by an authoritarian leader who embodies the highest ideals of the nation. This concept of the leader as hero or superman, borrowed in part from the romanticism of Friedrich Nietzsche, Thomas Carlyle, and Richard Wagner, is closely linked with fascism's rejection of reason and intelligence and its emphasis on vision, creativeness, and "the will."

As a citizen of Nazi-occupied France, Ellul's experience with fascism was brutal and unmediated.

Ellul traveled to Germany in 1934 and 1935, on the invitation of certain Protestant associations. During his second visit, he even attended a Nazi gathering out of curiosity. It was then that he became fascinated at the ease with which "a crowd could be whipped up and welded into a

---

8. *Columbia Encyclopedia*, "Fascism."
9. Dear and Foot, "Fascism."
10. *Columbia Encyclopedia*, "Fascism."

single unit" devoted to the state.[11] During the war, he supported and served in the French Resistance against occupation by fascist Germany. Despite a half-hearted attempt to secure arms for his family and students living with them, he never took up arms, an act that Ellul suggests would have represented a surrender to necessity rather than an embrace of freedom. Interestingly, though, he insists that he was most tempted to take up arms as an International Brigadier opposing the fascist Nationalists in the Spanish Civil War. He claimed to have assisted in arming a number of combatants and notes that only his budding relationship with Yvette prevented him from joining the fight against Franco's forces.[12] Apparently, fascism and its evils inspired so much disdain from Ellul that he considered abandoning his convictions regarding nonviolent, but active, resistance.

Capitalism and Socialism

By the time Ellul wrote *Money and Power*, fascism had largely disappeared from the world stage. Two political economic systems vied for primacy in national and global politics: capitalism, paired with liberal democracy, and socialism. Capitalism entails the private ownership of the means of production—land and machines, for example—and their operation for profit, usually in competitive markets. The shape of allocation, production, distribution, and consumption is, for the most part, the result of aggregated individual preferences expressed through private transactions, which, theoretically, should put resources to their most productive uses and, in free markets with perfect information, create few transaction costs. In most of the developed world during the Cold War, capitalism was paired with democratic politics built upon free and fair elections and, sometimes, the constitutional separation of powers through a system of checks and balances that ensured that no one branch of government would be overly empowered vis-à-vis others.

Socialism, on the other hand, entails public ownership of the means of production and cooperative decisions about their use. Allocation, production, distribution, and consumption are, theoretically, public decisions taken in such a way as to maximize equity rather than production. Socialist states are always paired with a more or less dictatorial government that

---

11. Ellul, *Ellul on Religion, Technology, and Politics*, 63.
12. Ibid.

engages in central planning concerning investment, production, and consumption, making decisions theoretically reserved for "the public."

Ellul's opinions of capitalism and socialism were no higher than his opinion of fascism. Just as fascism offended Ellul's personalist commitments, he found both capitalism and socialism inherently dehumanizing. Capitalism, Ellul wrote, "has progressively subordinated all of life—individual and collective—to money."[13] Here it is worth quoting at length from *Money and Power*:

> Money has become the criterion for judging man and his activity. One by one the state, the legal system, art, and the churches have submitted to the power of money. This is the rule, not the exception, and it has nothing to do with corruption. As a matter of fact everyone has begun to think that money, the source of power and freedom, must take priority over everything else. This belief is well supported on the one hand by a general loss of spiritual sensitivity (if not of faith itself) and on the other by the incredible growth of technology.
>
> Looking at the material success that money has allowed us to achieve, how could anyone deny the excellence of money, the source of progress? Money, which allows us to obtain everything material progress offers (in truth, everything our fallen nature desires), is no longer merely an economic value. It has become a moral value and an ethical standard.
>
> We must recognize the truth in Karl Marx's observation that money, in the capitalist system, leads to alienation. One of the results of capitalism that we see developing throughout the nineteenth century is the subservience of being to having. This result makes allegiance to capitalism virtually impossible for a Christian. For it is not a by-product, something that might not have happened, a result that could be eliminated by a better organization of capitalism. To the contrary, it is the inevitable consequence of capitalism, for there is no other possibility when making money becomes the purpose of life.[14]

Ellul notes that capitalism *systematically* produces these outcomes. They are not the product of mismanagement or accident, but are inherent in the capitalist system itself. Preoccupation with money leads to the subordination of being to having.

---

13. Ellul, *Money and Power*, 20.
14. Ibid..

One might suspect that Ellul would be more sanguine about socialism. One would be wrong. As we have seen, despite his persistent affinity for the comprehensiveness of Marxist analysis, Ellul rejected Marxist ideology, especially in its most totalizing and globally ambitious forms. Even in theory, he found that these formulations were inimical to the Christian faith. However, he also had objections to practical aspects of actually existing socialism. As objectionable as he found the ethical challenges of capitalism, those of socialism were just as troubling. Just as capitalism resulted in a diminished humanity—people concerned with a narrowly economic range of human pursuits, John Stuart Mill's *homo economicus*[15]—socialism resulted in the same diminishment of humanity, which offended Ellul's more holistic sense of human personality. Ellul's disdain for socialism was at least as strong as his distaste for capitalism. In fact, he believed that socialism simply justified the intensification of what he found most distasteful about capitalism.

So Ellul was an equal-opportunity critic of every mainstream political fashion of his day, all of which were given to the pursuit of money and power. He had no patience for fascism and its subordination of truly human ends and means to the state. He had no sympathy for the love of money that he thought was an inherent and dehumanizing element of capitalism. And he thought that socialism intensified every bad thing about capitalism. How is it that Ellul's critiques of these three systems should seem so similar, not only in intensity, but in substance? And if these were deficient, to what political system would Ellul have recommended we subscribe?

Key Threads in Ellul's Analyses of Political Economic Systems

Ellul's strong reaction against fascism, capitalism, and socialism is accountable to key concepts in his analysis, which transcend these systems. While Ellul began his studies of political economic systems one alternative at a time, certain overarching categories and concerns guided his thought while at the same time helping focus his critique of each political economic system.[16] Ellul's critique of the state, money, and work found special places in his analyses of fascism, capitalism, and socialism, respectively.

---

15. Mill, "Definition of Political Economy," 137.
16. Ellul, *Ellul on Religion, Technology, and Politics*, 87.

The State and Totalitarianism

In an interview with Patrick Troude-Chastenet, Ellul notes that he did not "set out to make a global critique of the state."[17] Rather, he notes that he and his collaborator, Bernard Charbonneau, "based our critique of the state on what we saw happening before our very eyes during the thirties. There was the fascist state, the totalitarian state and so on, and then there was the recurring critique of the liberal state . . . Our critique was marked by historical manifestations of the state."[18] Asked whether, then, he was not decrying the state itself, he noted that the sum of his work brought him to a more systematic critique:[19]

> In the end we were [decrying the state, as such]. At first we criticized the fascist state, then the Hitlerian state then the Communist state and then, I remember our surprise and amazement when Charbonneau and I realized that after all the American state, with its capitalistic organization could be just as totalitarian, just as authoritarian and that it sucked people into its system just as the others did. In other words, our critique was the fruit of an experimental and historical observation and not at all theoretical or abstract.[20]

In the most obvious form of totalitarianism, fascist states required the subordination of the whole human person and condition to nationalist concerns. But Ellul came to believe that whether formally fascist, capitalist, or socialist, all modern states were totalitarian in ambition, if not always in fact. The modern state, a feature common to all forms of political economic organization with which Ellul was concerned, was problematic in and of itself.

Money and Necessity

Ellul viewed money in much the same way that he viewed the state: problematic in and of itself, regardless of the political economic system in which one operates. Money, he writes, has become an impersonal and abstract symbol of purchasing power that depends not on personal control but on

17. Ibid.
18. Ibid.
19. Ibid., 88.
20. Ibid.

"distant and complex interactions of which our acts are merely echoes."[21] Our distance from and lack of control over the production of purchasing power alienates us from responsibility. This means that the problems with money are

> impersonal and abstract . . . No need for any individual to make a decision, to question his or her own actions: money is simply a reality in one kind of economy. It is untouchable; the individual can do nothing about it. We each get our share of money. We spend it. What else can we do? If things do not go well, the most we can hope for is a change in the economy. And indeed, if money is an economic reality tightly linked to the social complex, what can we as individuals do when we see injustice, imbalance, disorder? In the presence of such an enormous machine, the individual act can hardly be taken seriously. . . . As soon as we accept the supremacy of global concerns and of the system, as soon as we agree that material conditions remove our freedom to choose, we absolve all individuals of all responsibility for their use of money.[22]

The pursuit of money is fundamentally an offense to freedom. Democratic capitalism actually surrenders the freedom that democracy supposes in favor of needing money to meet all of our needs, submitting to a Faustian bargain. Here Ellul echoes concerns expressed by Lewis Mumford in his article "Authoritarian and Democratic Technics":

> The bargain we are being asked to ratify takes the form of a magnificent bribe. Under the democratic-authoritarian social contract, each member of the community may claim every material advantage, every intellectual and emotional stimulus he may desire, in quantities hardly available hitherto even for a restricted minority: food, housing, swift transportation, instantaneous communication, medical care, entertainment, education. But on one condition: that one must not merely ask for nothing that the system does not provide, but likewise agree to take everything offered, duly processed and fabricated, homogenized and equalized, in the precise quantities that the system, rather than the person, requires. Once one opts for the system no further choice remains. In a word, if one surrenders one's life at source, authoritarian technics will give back as much of it as can be mechanically graded, quantitatively multiplied, collectively manipulated and magnified.[23]

21. Ellul, *Money and Power*, 10.
22. Ibid., 11–12.
23. Mumford, "Authoritarian and Democratic Technics," 6.

According to both Ellul and Mumford, the individual submits to the necessities and material demands created by impersonal forces seemingly beyond human control, so long as the system appears to offer everyone an opportunity for material benefit. Furthermore, according to Ellul, the abstraction of the system gives the impression that one does not make ethical decisions about how best to invest, spend, and save; one must play by the rules of a supposedly amoral system.

While the problem with money was most obvious in capitalist political economic systems, it was, according to Ellul, ubiquitous. Even socialist states submitted to the necessity of money. Tellingly, by the time that Ellul wrote an afterword to *Money and Power* in 1979, both China and Cuba had joined the Soviet Union in reestablishing money as a means of exchange, a store of value, and an incentive toward production.[24]

Work and Technique

If the totalitarian state was the chief problem of fascism and the necessity of money the chief problem of capitalism, then work as technique is the chief problem of socialism. As Ellul wrote:

> Socialism rightly attacks capitalism for subordinating man to money, for its unjust economic structures. Socialism takes for its motto "To each according to his work," which in communism becomes "To each according to his needs."
>
> This is all well and good. But how does socialism plan to achieve its goals? First, by strictly limiting human life to work, to economic activity. Everything else is superfluous, a superstructure made to give pleasure and happiness. Serious things have to do with work and production. It is even appropriate for people to work harder than ever before, because the future of socialism is tied to intense production.
>
> Of course we are positing honest socialist structures with a just distribution of goods and no unfair stockpiling. But even in such an ideal case we have organized life and society around the supremacy of the economic system. Individuals are still subordinated to their work, which itself is mandated by the needs of the world community. It is possible to say, without paradox, that socialism takes the worst features of capitalism and carries them to extremes while justifying them theoretically. In socialist society,

---

24. Ellul, *Money and Power*, 168.

> individuals are doubtless freed from subordination to others, such as capitalists, but they remain entirely submitted to production: the economy is the basis of their lives. This is precisely the source of real alienation—not the subservience of *being* to *personal having*, but the subservience of *being* to *doing* and to *collective having*.[25]

In socialism, work becomes the technique by which collective possession is achieved.

However, just as totalitarianism is not limited to fascism, nor the problem of money to capitalism, neither is the problem of work as technique limited to socialism. Furthermore, wherever it is found, the notion that work is virtuous because it produces security—whether in the form of individual or collective having—is contrary to the biblical narrative in which work that reflects necessity—the need to work in order to have—is a product of the fall and curse.

Ellul's preoccupations with the state and totalitarianism, money and necessity, and work and technique, are key features of his analysis of political economic systems. These threads are present throughout Ellul's work on political economic systems.

Ellul's Key Contribution: Justification, Idolatry, and Desacralization

Ellul's most important contribution to Christian thought about political economy are his concerns for justification, idolatry, and descralization. These are the predominant concerns of *Money and Power*.

Justification

In *Money and Power*, Ellul notes that people have become dependent upon political economic systems in order to justify themselves. Early in the book, he writes, "Whenever we talk about money, we always end up by asking, How should we organize the economy?—or even, What economic system should I support? 'At the moment,' we explain, 'I may not be using money the way I should, but when the new system (whatever it may be) is instituted, when the general money problem is solved, I in turn will become

---

25. Ibid., 21.

Politics and Economics

just.'"[26] He continues, noting that we have come to depend upon political economic systems to make us "right":

> When I want to talk about money, everyone hands me his system. "If there is a money problem, it is because the economic system is unsound." All we need to do to solve the money problem is to change the economic system. This amounts to predicting that man will become just and good, that he will know exactly what to do with his money, that he will no longer covet his neighbor's possessions, that he will no longer steal, that he will give up bribing women and public officials, that he will not be corrupted by his own material good fortune, that he will sympathize with the needy, that he will neither hoard his money nor waste it, that he will no longer dream of "upward mobility," that he will not use his accumulated wealth to gain power in society, that he will not use his money to humiliate others.[27]

Again along these lines, Ellul writes:

> Now collectivistic involvement makes it unnecessary to face up to our own situation. It is not useful to solve our own problems or to control ourselves; the individual act is unimportant. We can rest assured that our public activity will solve our own moral and spiritual problems as well as those of other people. We are therefore free to give in to all our sins, our injustice, our lust for money: these things are minor if we have joined the comforting system. Its public activity gives us our hope, our sole guarantee and, at the same time, our justification.
>
> For I am no longer just when I do good as an individual; by contrast, I am just (in my own eyes and those of my friends) when I have signed on the dotted line. I repeat, it matters little which system I join; they all have the same character. Thus I can continue to be extremely rich or to act like a scoundrel. If I have joined some social-justice system, both my money and my behavior are justified.

For Ellul, political economic systems are organized in such a way as to justify—to prove or qualify right, to show sufficient lawful reason for an action—relationships in human community. This drive toward justification by political economic technique is a key to understanding Ellul's critiques of fascist, capitalist, and socialist political economy.

26. Ibid., 11.
27. Ibid., 12.

Idolatry[28]

When we depend upon political economic systems—or anything else, for that matter—for our justification, then we are practicing idolatry. In Ellul's essay "Christian Faith and Social Reality," he states: "Technique is what it is. Administration, as a thing, is fine. The machine, as a thing, is fine. But as soon as people put their faith in this machine, place all their hope in this machine, are convinced that their spiritual life depends on this machine *and that actually the machine will be the vicarious instrument which will allow them cheaply to exercise love of neighbor, then at that moment, we are in full idolatry.*"[29] Notice that, for Ellul, when each of these things remains that which it was created to be, it is "fine." It is only when we begin to depend upon the machine, technique, or political system as the instrument by which we will outsource our love of neighbor that we become idolatrous. This idolatrous dimension is something that Ellul also refers to in *Money and Power*. According to Ellul, money is revealed in Scripture to be a test for the people of God: Will we worship mammon or Yahweh? We cannot worship both. More powerfully, political economic systems themselves are idols that we expect to solve all of our problems. This is Ellul's argument in *The Political Illusion*, in which he notes that, on the one hand, we expect that all problems have political solutions, and on the other hand, we expect that a properly ordered political economic system can provide everyone with the good life.[30]

From an Ellulian perspective, this idolatry explains the sheer deadliness of the twentieth century's political economic systems, for once we make a god of anything, we are prepared to make sacrifices to it: "What is tragic is that once a thing has been transformed into a divinity . . . we are ready to sacrifice persons to it. All the gods, we know from human history,

---

28. For Ellul, the concept of idolatry is an important one. It is most developed in his book *The New Demons*, the title of which may be more accurately translated as "The Newly Possessed." The book, largely a response to works by Dietrich Bonhoeffer and Harvey Cox, was a suggestion that the supposedly secular world was not, in fact, without gods that it worshipped. In *The New Demons*, Ellul is very clear that everyone will worship something. Whatever it is that serves as the organizing force in the thought and life of a person is the thing that person worships.

29. Ellul, "Christian Faith and Social Reality," 177. Emphasis added.

30. Ellul, *The Political Illusion*.

have demanded human sacrifice. With Technique, with the State, with the Fatherland, that continues."[31]

Desacralization and the Politics of Freedom

Ellul was opposed to the presumption that we could be justified by way of our political economic system. Instead, he believed that we should "desacralize," "desacramentalize," or "profane" the state, money, work, wealth, and power. As Joyce Main Hanks notes, "Ellul takes pleasure in reducing overblown concepts to their proper size."[32] In "Christian Faith and Social Reality," Ellul writes:

> Our ancestors, the first Christians, smashed the pagan idols . . . but now there is more. There are no more statues to break, but there are always idols. Now I believe that by smashing the religious character of this or that or these faces we liberate human beings. . . . When we desacralize in this way, we are also rendering a service to humankind because problems become much more simple to resolve when they are simply reasonable problems and when we do not attach passionate and religious values to them. However, this kind of profanation of the divinities of modern people must be done not only in words, not in doctrines and in theories, but must also penetrate practice. If we want to profane the divinity of money, for Christians there is a simple means, and the Bible gives us only one, which is to give. You want your money to cease being a god, you have a means: give it. To profane the state, affirm the liberty of the person and your own liberty in actions—actions in the face of the decisions that can make an idol of the state. It might even mean, under certain conditions, refusing to participate in political life. I do not say always, all the time, but under certain conditions; sometimes, to be a good, and true, and loyal citizen might mean refusing to play the game that the state offers us.[33]

Our acts of desacralization do not have only this negative aspect. They also have a positive aspect, which one might describe as the "politics of freedom." Our desacralization of money and power, in showing that the wealth and the state are not gods, also demonstrates our freedom in the face of necessity and the freedom of the one true God to justify whom he freely

31. Ellul, "Christian Faith and Social Reality," 177.
32. Hanks, "Politics of God," 218.
33. Ellul, "Christian Faith and Social Reality," 176–78.

chooses. As Ellul writes in *Money and Power*, "We are called to use our wealth so that our actions announce to the watching world that election is free, that grace is abundant, that a new creation is promised, and that God owns all things."[34]

The Politics of God: The Politics of Freedom

This, then, is what Ellul was *for*. If he was *against* every political economic system of his time, he was *for* a politics of freedom. And this did not suggest a separatist movement. On the contrary, Christians should involve themselves in politics. In his book *The Politics of God and the Politics of Man*, Ellul reflected deeply on insights from the Old Testament for contemporary political thought. He wrote that the concern of 2 Kings with Israel "genuinely constituted as a political power and playing its part in the concert of empires" is not "unimportant to those who think the political problem should not be discussed in the church."[35] To those who suggest that the church should not be involved with politics, Ellul writes, "The Bible shows us that the church is not just a spiritual matter, that politics is not just simply a human action of no concern to us. It may be that politics is the kingdom of the devil, but this certainly concerns us as Christians."[36] Politics, like technique and the city, might be part of the world's efforts to reject God, but that does not mean that Christians should avoid it. Rather, Christians should involve themselves with a specific interest in and intention to descracalize politics—to show that it is not absolute. Just as Ellul writes against those who think that the church should shy away from politics, he writes against those who seem to think that politics is the ultimate concern: "This meditation is also not unimportant in the face of those who want politics to be the main action of men, and of Christians who think involvement in politics is *essential* and for whom everything is finally politics. In fact, [2 Kings] shows the *relativity* of politics."[37] When Christians involve themselves in politics, they should do so in such a way as reveals the relativity of politics in the face of the claim that politics is absolute, and the absoluteness of God in the face of the claim that God is relative.

34. Ellul, *Money and Power*, 68.
35. Ellul, *Politics of God*, 13.
36. Ibid.
37. Ibid.

In other words, we should involve ourselves lightly in the affairs of politics. For Ellul, Christians should not disengage from politics. Nor should they regard involvement in politics as essential. Christians should not seek to create a Christian state, and they should not disengage from politics either. Rather, Christians should involve themselves in such a way as demonstrates that any given political position or economic system, while it may be useful or even preferable over alternatives, is not essential. By demonstrating this *through a peculiar posture of engagement*, Christians bear witness to the fact that God alone is absolute and essential.

CHAPTER 6

Scripture

> "*Every living word of God cannot be different from that which is attested precisely in the Bible. . . . It turns out that the God who spoke to men in the Bible is also our God, and directly ours, thanks to their witness.*"[1]

READERS WHO ENCOUNTER JACQUES Ellul through his sociological works are sometimes surprised to learn that he wrote so extensively about the Bible. Ellul endorsed and practiced the "theological interpretation of Scripture" or "theological exegesis" decades before there emerged a renaissance of academic interest in such an approach to the Bible. This contemporary scholarly movement has spawned a spate of monographs, an expansive dictionary, a commentary series, and a specialized academic journal, which together share in common the lofty aim of enabling Christian communities to "hear the word of God in Scripture and hence to be transformed by the renewing of their minds (Rom 12:2)."[2]

For all its variety, this ecumenical movement of experts in biblical studies and theology shares the assumption that the Bible is a unified and cohesive whole, comprised of Old and New Testaments, which are upheld together as Christian Scripture. The Bible constitutes authoritative revelation from God, and its entirety bears witness to the Good News of Jesus Christ. The Scriptures are to be read and interpreted from the standpoint

---

1. Ellul, *To Will and to Do*, 274n1.
2. Vanhoozer, "Introduction," 22. For more on this movement, see Treier, *Introducing Theological Interpretation*; Fowl, *Theological Interpretation*; and Billings, *The Word of God for the People of God*; see also *The Journal of Theological Interpretation*, established in 2007.

of the confessional commitments of the church, for the sake of nurturing Christian faith and practice through "coming to hear God's word and to know God better."[3] This movement insists that its approach to interpretation is best suited to the Bible's own account of its nature and purpose. According to Spinks, interpretations of Scripture that are self-consciously "theological" are ones that "consciously seek to do justice to the perceived theological nature of the texts and embrace the influence of theology (corporate and personal; past and present) upon the interpreter's enquiry, context, and method."[4]

Similarly, Ellul's understanding of Scripture and its interpretation exemplifies an unapologetically theological approach to reading the Bible. Following the lead of Karl Barth, Ellul has a high view of Scripture as divine revelation; Scripture is God speaking to humanity through the text. He wrote: "It is clear that every living word of God cannot be different from that which is attested precisely in the Bible . . . It turns out that the God who spoke to men in the Bible is also our God, and directly ours, thanks to their witness."[5] Even more boldly, Ellul asserts that "the Bible is the objectified datum both of what has been revealed and what is potentially revealed."[6] The written Word of God in Scripture bears witness to the incarnate Word of God, Jesus Christ, who is the focus of the entire revelation. The rationale for this view is found in various places in the New Testament, perhaps most notably in Luke 24. Speaking to his disciples on the road to Emmaus after his resurrection, Jesus, "beginning with Moses and all the Prophets . . . explained to them what was said in all the Scriptures concerning himself" (Luke 24:27). Accordingly, Ellul advocates a Christ-centered ("christocentric") approach to biblical interpretation: "It is impossible to ignore the fact of the unity of revelation and its movement. Everything leads to Jesus Christ, just as everything comes from him."[7] Ellul follows Barth in insisting that the written Word in Scripture is always a *living* word, which is spoken to those who receive that word by faith. He wrote: "The word read in the Bible cannot be heard as a personal commandment except by faith."[8]

---

3. Vanhoozer, "Introduction," 22.
4. Spinks, *Bible and the Crisis of Meaning*, 7.
5. Ellul, *To Will and to Do*, 274n1.
6. Ellul, *Ethics of Freedom*, 161.
7. Ellul, *Politics of God*, 9.
8. Ellul, *Prayer and Modern Man*, 116.

Ellul does not think there is a single, "correct" method of interpreting Scripture (and even does not rule out some use of allegorical methods). He recognizes the importance of "wrestling" with the biblical text "to get at its contents by every human method possible: exegesis, criticism, analysis."[9] Indeed, Ellul's own works of biblical exposition interact extensively with such scholarly efforts by professional Bible scholars. Not surprisingly, he is sharply critical of "modern hermeneutics" on account of "its complete subjection to the modern cultural background with its fashions and fads and scientific façade and ideology."[10] He rejects the notion that the Bible simply is a historical artifact, to be read like any other ancient book, and therefore is concerned "only to show how the text is constituted" in light of genre, ancient backgrounds, and literary forms. From his standpoint, this approach "has no bearing on the better understanding of the matter of the text. The sense is not made apparent by an explanation of the manner or origin."[11] Often, he says, "the sense is reduced to a few grains of dust or to nothing at all."[12] He calls this practice the "dissolution" of the text, which "strips the text of its meaning" by isolating specific texts "from the sense of the revelation."[13]

Three features of Ellul's critique are important to notice. First, Ellul rejects a reductionistic mentality. Interpreters who dissect biblical texts into smaller and smaller fragments are likely to lose sight of the meaning of the Bible. Second, he believes that Christian interpreters should have a different attitude toward their work, one that does not adopt fashionable but unworthy assumptions about their efforts. At bottom, his critique is that "hermeneutics is the business of interpreting revelation without revelation."[14] Thus, the Christian affirmation of Scripture as revealed truth should make a difference to how we read the Bible. Third, we need to notice that for Ellul, the goal of biblical interpretation is discerning the *matter* (that is, its subject or substance) and the *sense* of the biblical text (that is, the meaning or message).

Ellul's positive account of Christian interpretation begins with the assumption that a Christian's methods should be consistent with the nature of

---

9. Ellul, *Ethics of Freedom*, 166.
10. Ibid., 162.
11. Ibid., 179.
12. Ibid.
13. Ellul, *Hope in Time of Abandonment*, 142.
14. Ibid., 146.

Scripture as "revealed truth."[15] At this point, Ellul has clear similarities with Dietrich Bonhoeffer, who wrote, "Theological exposition takes the Bible as the book of the church and interprets it as such. This is its presupposition and this presupposition constitutes its method; its method is a continual returning from the text (as determined by all the methods of philological and historical research) to this presupposition."[16] Working from the assumption of Scripture as revelation, there is a properly faithful way of using the intellectual tools of historical-critical exegesis. Deployed in faith and for faith, they are oriented toward "the glory of God and love of neighbor."[17] Genuinely Christian biblical interpretation is a matter of using the available resources of learning in order to enable people "to see in this document of revelation a new depth of God's love and so communicate it as to bring them to the truth."[18] He sees this task of biblical interpretation as central to the church's life and witness in the modern world: "What is at stake in theological research is the ability of believers to live out and to confess their faith in the midst of their human responsibilities."[19] The goal of biblical and theological study should be to "purify the faith that we confess, since we are always tempted to put the Word into images or idols." Following Barth, he writes, "The mission of research is to denounce our false interpretations of God and to clear away that which serves as the envelope of our preaching and theology."[20] For Ellul, theology is best understood and practiced as being undertaken from within the fellowship of the church and for the sake of "the witness of the gospel to the world."[21]

In the sections that follow, we will examine his understanding of Genesis 1–3, Jonah, Ecclesiastes, and Revelation.

Genesis 1–3

Our discussion of Ellul's interpretation of Genesis 1–3 is drawn from several sources. A valuable recent addition to our knowledge of Ellul is the transcription of Ellul's 1974 Bible study sessions on these chapters, held in

15. Ellul, *Ethics of Freedom*, 182.
16. Bonhoeffer, *Creation and Fall*, 22.
17. Ellul, *Ethics of Freedom*, 166.
18. Ibid., 167.
19. Ibid., 176.
20. Ibid., 178.
21. Ibid., 176.

his home.[22] In addition, we will examine four essays by Ellul that deal with the implications of Genesis 1–3 for our understandings of work, vocation, and technology.

The opening chapters of Genesis are extraordinarily complex texts that not only have proven controversial but also have been interpreted in vastly conflicting ways over the centuries. Ellul begins his account of Genesis 1 by discussing the concept of biblical inspiration. He claims that God's revelation of himself to people does not reduce the human authors of Scripture to "dictaphones. They hear and respond as the people they are with their means, their knowledge, their language, and their culture."[23] Thus, Ellul's approach wishes to take seriously what the ancient writers were attempting to say, given their intellectual frameworks, and he resists the imposition of modern or "scientific" paradigms. Likewise, Ellul rejects the imposition of metaphysical categories: "One of the biggest mistakes has been the transformation of the Bible into a metaphysics."[24] He explains that "the problem is that Greek philosophy asks questions to which the Bible does not in the least seek to reply."[25] The Greeks were interested in the "origin of the world," but Genesis is not. Genesis 1 should not be read as a "metaphysics" of creation, because it "is about something else entirely."[26]

All this is quite tantalizing, but what then is Genesis 1–3 really about? Ellul holds that the biblical authors "were not searching for historical objectivity" and that the text of Genesis 1 is "not trying to tell us objectively what exactly happened, but instead, what it means."[27] It is not an account of "facts" nor "a cosmogony" but "a teaching about the God who revealed himself to Israel. This is something totally different."[28] Already we can see Ellul operating as a theological interpreter of Scripture since his focus is on the Bible's teaching about the nature and character of *God*. Adopting the critical hypothesis of diverse literary sources for the early chapters of Genesis, Ellul focuses on the divine names Elohim (used in Genesis 1) and Yahweh (used in Genesis 2) in order to emphasize that the Bible's own purpose is to describe God's relationship to the world, and to humanity, through his

22. Ellul, *Freedom, Love, and Power*.
23. Ibid., 5.
24. Ibid., 6.
25. Ibid., 8.
26. Ibid., 6.
27. Ibid., 11.
28. Ibid., 18.

Scripture

Word. Ellul's emphasis is that the creation narrative is about God's provision of the world in which human beings will live in relationship with God.

Particularly important for our purposes in this book is Ellul's concept of the image of God, which first appears in Gen 1:27–28. He rejects the idea that the image of God refers to some specific capacity (e.g., free will, intelligence). Instead he emphasizes the Bible's references to the image of God being male and female, "his being two in one," so that "humanity is the only being created as one person separated into two forms."[29] Thus, "he-and-she cannot be thought of in themselves, independent from the One of whom he-and-she is the image." Human beings are made for relationship; more specifically, "he-and-she" are made for sharing love. Again, relational language dominates Ellul's approach. His most original interpretation is that the image of God is love. He realizes that the word *love* never occurs explicitly in these texts, but he insists that the meaning of the text is best expressed by that terminology.[30] As a creature, human beings are made by God with "an ability to respond" to God, particularly by entering into dialogue with God.[31] This point has paramount importance for Ellul, since "freedom is a prerequisite for love."[32] Indeed, "theologically speaking, freedom and love are indissociably linked."[33]

Given the centrality of freedom in Ellul's thought, and the importance of his strict opposition of freedom and necessity, we need to notice that the primacy of freedom is found in his understanding of the *imago dei*, and therefore is foundational to his entire reading of Scripture. God's gift of freedom means, for Ellul, that "God submits himself to human initiatives."[34] Thus, "God withdraws in order to leave the field free for humanity."[35] This stance gives human history an immense significance; it even leads Ellul to deny the idea of divine providence, in the sense that "God does not step by step, minute by minute, dictate what is to happen in the world, thereby establishing the reality of that world, as it were."[36]

---

29. Ellul, *Freedom, Love, and Power*, 30.
30. Ibid.
31. Ibid., 32.
32. Ibid., 31.
33. Ibid., 53.
34. Ibid., 35.
35. Ibid., 37.
36. Ibid.

Taking Genesis 1–2 in this way, Ellul believes that the early chapters of Genesis must be understood as carrying "existential" meaning: they describe the realities of human existence in God's world: "They seek to reveal who humanity is, including its relationship to God."[37] He resists the idea that we can derive an abstract concept of "human nature" from such an account or derive "any moral obligations" from it. Instead, the text describes the freedom given to human beings to respond to God in love. Human beings "rule" over creation "so that humanity can bring to God the love of the whole of that creation. It is the primary vocation that the text attributes to humanity."[38] The notion of freedom becomes central to his exposition of relationship with God and his account of the fall (a term he dislikes, preferring to speak of "the rupture" or "break" between humans and God). Ellul denies that the Bible gives an explanation of the origin of evil, preferring to say that "it is intended to help us take what might be called an existential position," by which Ellul means the Scripture enables one to find a coherent way to live out one's faith amidst the realities of evil.[39] Genesis 3 teaches us, according to Ellul, that the "break" with God was caused by humanity's desire for its independence from God. Rather than living out freedom in love through communion with the Creator, humanity exercised its freedom by choosing to say "No" to God. The text reveals a "fundamental truth that reaches to the very heart of our lives, instead of telling us the factual details."[40] In our chapter on Ellul's approach to ethics, we will explore the importance of the "break" with God for human moral knowledge.

There is much more that could be said about Ellul's account of Genesis 1–3. For our purposes in this book, however, it is essential to notice his view of work, before and after the "break" with God. This is the theological basis for his sociological and historical view of technology and technique. Ellul offers some interestingly idiosyncratic comments on Gen 2:15, "The LORD God took the man and put him in the Garden of Eden to work it and take care of it." He states: "Humanity is called to render a service, but one that is useless."[41] He believes that the garden "did not need to be cultivated since it was fruitful, and it did not need to be guarded since there were no

---

37. Ellul, *Freedom, Love, and Power*, 33.
38. Ibid., 35.
39. Ibid., 61.
40. Ibid., 72. Ellul does not interpret Gen 1–3 as dealing with "scientific historical investigation."
41. Ibid., 51.

Scripture

external enemies. This is exactly the point: there is no necessity to work and there is no necessity to be productive. All there is, is the Word of God."[42] According to Ellul, this is simply a matter of doing what God says, no matter how absurd it might be, simply because what God says must be good. The text therefore is not about what he calls "real work" and cannot provide any theological basis for a positive Christian account of the spiritual value of work in the sense of our daily occupations.

In a provocative essay, Ellul argues this point in more detail. He contends that the work that God gave humans to do before the fall was not the sort of work that involves technique. He reasons that the creation was "perfect and finished" through God's own work, hence, there was nothing that human work could add to it. Whatever "work" was being done in "cultivating" the garden, it was "not work to gather a surplus, to make a living, to produce: it was work for nothing."[43] In other words, it was not work done because something had to be done, work out of necessity; instead work was "a free action that was hardly different from play."[44] Ellul's most important conclusion is this: "The entire world of techniques in all their applications was completely foreign to Eden."[45] Since God provided everything for his creatures, there would have been no necessity and no existential drive toward efficiency; tools of industry and convenience were unknown in the prelapsarian state. In the conclusion of his essay, Ellul seeks to clarify that he

> did not say that technique is a fruit of sin. I did not say that technique is contrary to the will of God. I did not say that technique in itself is evil. I said only that technique is not a prolongation of the Edenic creation, that it is not a compliance of man to a vocation that was given to him by God, that it is not the fruit of the first nature of Adam. It is the product of the situation in which sin has put man; it is inscribed exclusively in a fallen world; it is uniquely part of this fallen world; it is a product of necessity and not of human freedom.[46]

While Ellul stops just short of claiming that the whole phenomenon of technique is a result of sin, he does paint an idyllic picture of prelapsarian work in Eden as essentially nonwork, since "real work" in his sense

---

42. Ellul, *Freedom, Love, and Power*, 51.
43. Ellul, "Technique and the Opening Chapters of Genesis," 126.
44. Ibid., 127.
45. Ibid., 129.
46. Ibid., 135.

must inevitably be dominated by technique. By associating technique with the fallen, sinful world, and by distancing technique from God's created purposes, in theological terms it becomes very hard to give any positive account of human "work" in a meaningful sense of the term, and very hard to see how "technique" can be redeemed from the taint of sin. This approach sets the theological groundwork for what many critics have seen as a pessimistic view of technique, technology, and work.

Jonah

Ellul's *Le Livre de Jonas* (literally, "The Book of Jonah") was written in 1952. As such, it was the author's third book, following *The Theological of Foundation of Law* (1946) and *The Presence of the Kingdom* (1948). The English translation did not appear until 1971 with the title, *The Judgment of Jonah*. This work has received wildly differing evaluations. According to Brevard Childs, an eminent Old Testament scholar from Yale, "Jacques Ellul's short monograph on Jonah is far more akin to the genre of sermon than commentary. Probably the book will satisfy neither the left nor the right in the traditional theological spectrum, but it represents a highly creative, robust theological interpretation which cannot but stimulate serious reflection."[47] On the other hand, Lloyd R. Bailey witheringly concludes that Ellul's treatment is "illogical, theologically trite, and critically uninformed. Those who have not yet paid $1.95 for it may consider themselves fortunate."[48]

What provokes such strong and divergent reactions? A clue comes from the book's translator, Geoffrey Bromiley, who calls the work "an existential commentary" and explains: "above all, this is a theological or more specifically a Christological commentary. The author's chief aim is to relate the book, not to Christians, but to Christ. Ellul thinks Christ is the center of all Scripture and he also takes seriously the specific reference which Christ makes to the sign of Jonah. If this reading is correct, and the Bible is indeed a unity, the exposition of Ellul, though not developed in detail, has a distinctive theological contribution to make."[49] Ellul does not offer anything like the average historical-critical commentary, which moves verse by verse through the text, with special attention to Hebrew words, grammatical constructions, and specifics of the ancient background context. His driving

---

47. Childs, *Old Testament Books*, 86.
48. Bailey, review of *Judgment of Jonah*, 174.
49. Bromiley, "Translator's Preface," 5.

concerns are far more thematic, seeking to elicit the theological message of the book. Although critics may dislike some of the exegetical details of Ellul's interpretation, the basic sticking point is whether a reader accepts his boldly Christ-centered way of understanding Jonah.

Ellul's resolutely theological reading of Jonah is not particularly interested in questions about whether Jonah is historically accurate. Did Jonah really get swallowed up by a fish? This is a matter of "secondary" importance for Ellul, because "the story finds its true value not in itself, in what it is, but in what it denotes. Its relevance derives from the truth which it embodies, from the one who fulfills the prophecy."[50] Ellul takes very seriously that the book is a prophetic book, and he attributes critical significance to its placement within the prophetic works, not the historical books, of the Hebrew canon of Scripture. As a prophetic book, Ellul takes it as speaking about future events to unfold in subsequent revelation and to be recorded in the New Testament. Thus, "it is in the light of Jesus Christ that the story is true and Jonah concerns us."[51] What matters for Ellul is the "spiritual meaning" of divine revelation in God's word. "God's word in the story has value, not the miracle as such."[52]

Ellul's way of approaching Jonah is bound to be controversial since he employs from start to finish what biblical scholars call a typological method. According to Daniel Treier, typology is a kind of "Christ-centered" reading that recognizes that "both particular Old Testament persons and Israel the people of God anticipate Christ by being divine action with a human vocation."[53] The main idea is that events in the Old Testament are seen as prefiguring New Testament events, especially events in the life of Jesus.

In line with this way of reading, Ellul states: "Jonah is a figure, a type of Christ. To prove this one has only to consider that Jesus referred the revelation of Jonah to himself."[54] For instance, Ellul believes that Jonah's descent into the "abyss" of the fish's belly prefigures what Jesus experienced. "What happens to Jonah happens to Jesus."[55] Just as Jonah suffers isolation from

---

50. Ellul, *Judgment of Jonah*, 17. Later on, Ellul comments on the story of the fish swallowing Jonah, saying that "the chief aim of the story is not to give historical information, even though the miracle of the fish is quite acceptable, and I for my part see no objection to the possibility of a miracle of this kind" (ibid., 45).

51. Ibid., 37.

52. Ibid., 62.

53. Treier, "Typology," 826.

54. Ellul, *Judgment of Jonah*, 17.

55. Ibid., 59.

God, so does Jesus in his suffering and death. And just as God brought Jonah out of the depth of hell in the fish's belly, so God raised Jesus from the depth of hell.[56]

Moreover, Ellul believes that the book of Jonah pertains not only to the Israelites of the Old Testament, but to the church, "whose relations to God are still of the same type as those of ancient Israel."[57] Thus, Ellul seeks to draw out the significance of the book for the contemporary church. "In Jonah we see a man who is like us, who has reactions like ours, whose revolts and sins are ours."[58] In fact, Ellul sees the book of Jonah as a book that speaks fundamental truths about the human relationship to God. "It records the attitudes of all men when they receive God's call and are in the presence of his grace."[59] In particular, Ellul takes the occasion of Jonah to reflect on the meaning of divine election, that is, God's choice of certain individuals to participate in his work. When God sends Jonah to Nineveh, he flees, rejecting the assignment that comes from God and breaking away from God's people in the process. Ellul sees this as a universal feature: "the story of Jonah is indeed the story of all of us."[60] Jonah's disobedience points toward the unfaithfulness of the church, which often fails to obey God's call. Just as Jonah is called to join in God's work of salvation by preaching to the nations, so too the church sadly fails its missional calling on many occasions. Ellul develops the theme that the church's calling consists in serving others, taking one's own part in God's work in the world, since "God needs man" to accomplish his purposes. "If Jonah receives a call, if he is truly saved, it is for others. From the moment faith develops in us, we must be permeated by the conviction that if grace is conferred on us it is primarily for others. It is never for our own personal satisfaction."[61]

Ellul's way of understanding the great fish actually stands on reasonable exegetical grounds. He argues that the fish is not a sign of grace, since the "fish was sent primarily to swallow up, to destroy, to put to death. It was not a means of saving."[62] Rather, the fish represents hell. Jonah has "traversed the agony and death and come to this hell prepared by God to en-

---

56. Ibid., 60. Cf. Matt 12:39–42.
57. Ellul, *Judgment of Jonah*, 16.
58. Ibid., 72.
59. Ibid., 16.
60. Ibid., 28.
61. Ibid., 89.
62. Ellul, *Judgment of Jonah*, 43.

force the total separation of man and God."⁶³ Thus, "what Jonah encounters is absolute hell."⁶⁴ The miracle of Jonah's deliverance is reflected in what Jonah actually says from inside the fish, namely, he addresses God from the standpoint of a fresh experience of God's grace. Jonah praises God for the deliverance, salvation, and reconciliation with God that he discovered. This teaches all people about the reality of spiritual death in separation from God and brings the reminder of the reality of God's presence. "God is with Jonah in the belly of the fish."⁶⁵ In fact, Ellul even says that Jonah "announces as a prophet that Jesus himself has come where he is."⁶⁶ The story of Jonah underscores the reality of God's love, expressed not only in saving Jonah but in sparing Nineveh, which Ellul understands to stand for "the world" in general. In the closing sections of his exposition, Ellul highlights God's patience, a lovingkindness that withholds judgment and bestows grace.

Ecclesiastes

Ellul's three-hundred-page interpretation of the Old Testament book of Ecclesiastes, written in 1987 under the title, *La raison d'être: Méditation sur l'Ecclésiaste*, appeared in English translation in 1990 as *The Reason for Being: A Meditation on Ecclesiastes*. Ellul begins the book with a revealing personal statement:

> I am no scholar or exegete, neither interpreter nor theologian. My only qualification is that I have read, meditated on, and prayed over Ecclesiastes for more than fifty years. I have probably explored it more than any other book in the Bible. It has perhaps given me more, spoken to me more, than any other. We could say that I am now committing this dialogue to writing.⁶⁷

This statement has three implications for our study. First, it reveals Ellul's self-understanding in approaching Scripture. It was not false humility that led him to deny being an exegete. He read the Old Testament in Hebrew, and pored over a dozen technical commentaries by leading scholars in the process of writing this work. In terms of the academic guild, he was not a

63. Ibid., 44.
64. Ibid., 45.
65. Ibid., 55.
66. Ibid.
67. Ellul, *Reason for Being*, 1.

professional biblical interpreter or theologian, but a layman whose interests resided in the contemporary application of the text's message as divine revelation. Second, Ellul's remark suggests just how deeply a lifetime of biblical reflection shaped his entire outlook. It would be hard to overestimate the extent to which Ellul is a biblical thinker: his social and political analysis is the product of a mind steeped in the Bible's way of thinking. His originality as a sociologist, historian or even philosopher is the result of bringing a particular theological perspective to his work, even if that perspective usually operates mostly in the background of his social interpretation. Those readers who wish to engage Ellul's "secular" writings without studying his "religious" works put themselves at a severe disadvantage and thereby risk misunderstanding Ellul. Third, this comment suggests how deeply Ecclesiastes in particular has shaped his outlook. Those who are quite familiar with Ellul's temperament, corpus, and dialectical mode of thought should not be surprised that a mostly overlooked and deeply paradoxical sample of ancient Hebrew Wisdom Literature has played such a formative role.

Ellul offers what he calls "a modern meditation on Ecclesiastes."[68] He said that he considered *The Presence of the Kingdom* a "general introduction to all of what I wanted to write" and considered his book on Ecclesiastes his "last word" (even though he wrote several books after it).[69] His meditation provides some rather pointed criticisms of traditional biblical scholarship. He resists the "instinct in almost all exegetes of Ecclesiastes" to "prove that this text is like any other."[70] In particular, he is critical of attempts to fit Ecclesiastes into previously established frameworks, even the assumption of "formal, logical coherence." For Ellul, there is a distinctive logic within Ecclesiastes that interpreters have missed and that a careful reader should discern. This involves a committed reading, a stance of submission to the truth of the text, which characterizes what is now being called "theological interpretation" of the Bible. For Ellul, because "we are dealing with texts considered holy, bearers of revelation, we cannot exactly treat them with the benevolent neutrality appropriate for an ordinary literary text."[71] He presses for a deeper engagement with the message of Ecclesiastes. With characteristic boldness, he opines: "The thing that most surprised me in the majority of Ecclesiastes commentators was their extraordinary knowledge

68. Ibid., 3.
69. Ibid., 4.
70. Ibid., 8.
71. Ibid.

of Hebrew, coupled with the superficiality of their thought."[72] He finds them guilty of an "utter lack of comprehension" due to a "total lack of interest and research" about the *meaning* of the text. For Ellul, the book's focus is a theological message: "the proclamation of the unique and transcendent God, whose presence is the meaning, the purpose, the origin, and the end of the entire work."[73] For him, "the reference to God is central; that is to say, decisive and pivotal."[74] At the same time, he insists that Ecclesiastes offers a diagnosis of the universal human condition. Because it is a divinely inspired writing, Ellul believes that it speaks to "all people" about life while offering us "truth concerning God."[75]

Ellul's interpretive approach hinges upon a very sophisticated, and entirely plausible, account of the literary structure of Ecclesiastes. The book displays a deep internal coherence, but not one that represents "rational Western logic."[76] He argues that "the coherence of this text stems from a kind of woven texture rather than a logical plan, and I believe that I can perceive a texture in Qohelet like that of a complex variegated piece of cloth."[77] Ellul identifies two major themes: vanity and wisdom.

> They contradict each other. Wisdom is subjected to vanity, true! But wisdom also constitutes our only weapon against vanity. We witness a kind of debate between wisdom and vanity. On the one hand, wisdom demonstrates the vanity of everything, but is itself vanity. On the other hand, vanity loses its sharpness and bitterness, since the wise person has passed beyond all vanity. At this point, we begin to see one of the possibilities of Qohelet. But the book does not limit itself to this immanent and uncontrollable circle, since it also refers to God.[78]

The book features an internal dialogue between vanity and wisdom, an alternation that is flatly contradictory, punctuated by sections about God. For instance, happiness is fleeting and worthless, yet all a person can do is live as happily as possible. These contradictions are deliberate on the part of the author, whom Ellul refers to as Qohelet. These are the key to the

---

72. Ellul, *Reason for Being*, 12.
73. Ibid., 22.
74. Ibid., 37.
75. Ibid., 33.
76. Ibid., 34.
77. Ibid., 36. See Ellul's diagram of the book's structure on page 38.
78. Ibid., 36.

entire work, in order to convey the central message: "human existence is essentially self-contradictory."[79] For Ellul, the whole "mode of thinking" in Ecclesiastes is geared around the "principle of contradiction."[80] He argues that "the meaning of the text resides precisely *in* the contradiction."[81] Thus, the literary techniques of irony and paradox dominate its pages.

Ellul's book is organized thematically (rather than sequentially) around the central threads of the "woven texture" of Ecclesiastes. A chapter on vanity reviews the core idea of vanity (which he sees fundamentally as uselessness), the myth of progress or historical development, power or domination, money, work, pleasure, and happiness. All these features of human life are nothing more than "chasing after wind." The topic of work illustrates the paradoxical nature of Qohelet's teaching: "all is vanity; all human work is vanity. But whatever your hand finds to do, do it! In other words, do not worry about its being vanity; do not try to guess whether it is useful."[82] The function of these texts, for Ellul, is "to establish that for Qohelet (in reality, for the whole Bible) the real human adventure begins on the basis of the radical thought that 'all is vanity.' It begins when we realize that basically nothing has any use, when all our illusions have been stripped away."[83] Yet, despite this apparently gloomy analysis, Ecclesiastes is not a "book of despair" but is "part of the Good News" of Jesus Christ.[84]

Ellul's next chapter deals with wisdom and philosophy. The key point is that human wisdom is also subject to vanity and thus comes to nothing. Ecclesiastes' negative and paradoxical analysis of life does not lead the reader to conclude that wisdom provides a satisfying answer that solves our existential problems or provides meaning amidst what appears meaningless. Rather, Qohelet's discussion leads the reader to seek perspective from God, not from human wisdom. For instance, Qohelet's denunciation of words and their lack of power leads the reader to the exhortation to "fear God" (Eccl 5:7), and the discussion of possessions and wealth leads to a reference to "the work of God, the Maker of all things" (Eccl 11:5). For Ellul, Qohelet's point is that "every road brings us back to this decisive

79. Ibid.
80. Ibid., 40.
81. Ibid.
82. Ibid., 102.
83. Ibid., 116.
84. Ibid., 118.

Scripture

point: what God does."[85] In the face of the vanity of life and the failure of human wisdom, the book of Ecclesiastes offers, "But I say" and makes an affirmation or proclamation about God, without attempting "to convince us through reason of the existence or reality of God."[86]

Thus, in a concluding chapter on God, Ellul points out that there are over thirty significant references to God, always cited with the Hebrew word *Elohim* as the source of universal wisdom. He adds: "if you remove everything about God in this book, thinking to produce a text on secular wisdom, you utterly dismember it."[87] Ellul emphasizes that God cannot be "used" by us to solve our problems, such as the existential problems of evil or suffering. The main theme concerning God is that God is a generous giver of gifts, which are to be received with gratitude, as all of life is referred back to God, even amidst the perplexities and vanities of everyday existence. Work is meaningless. Paradoxically, happiness in work is still possible, but only as a gift from God: "finding satisfaction in all of their toil—this is a gift from God" (Eccl 3:13).[88]

For Ellul, the fundamental contribution of Ecclesiastes is the provision of a perspective for life. He comments: "Qohelet does not say that things 'are,' but that he sees or conceives them in a certain way . . . 'I interpret this as a gift from God'; someone else may see something else in it or nothing at all. No matter."[89] This is the biblical manner of affirming that "wisdom comes from God. It lies nowhere else, has no independence. It leads to nothing but smoke, mist, wind, and vanity. But it becomes wisdom, perhaps the same wisdom, beginning at the moment the sage recognizes it to be in God's hand—another gift of God."[90] From this standpoint, Ellul refers to a distinction which he developed in *The Humiliation of the Word* between reality and truth:

> How can [Qohelet] express on the one hand an implacable realism that never lets up and never tries to escape, yet on the other hand avoid despair or excess? I believe he provides us with a model of what a person in God's grasp can understand and know of humanity and society. God is Mystery. But this living God acts on a

85. Ellul, *Reason for Being*, 205.
86. Ibid., 212.
87. Ibid., 214.
88. Ibid., 256.
89. Ibid., 258.
90. Ibid., 277.

> person, places him in a new situation, and from the situation, the person can see himself, others, and this world. He can see at the same time the *reality* of things as they are (this constitutes his realism) and also their *truth* (i.e., he can see their profound existence before God and for God). In this case, reality prevents truth from being an escape into the clouds or into dreams . . . And truth prevents reality from turning into despair, from leading a person to skepticism, then to nihilism, and finally and unfailingly, to suicide.
>
> In reality, all is vanity. In truth, everything is a gift of God. This represents Qohelet's position, as I understand it.[91]

For Ellul, the book's concluding words are profoundly forceful and truly the climax: "Fear God and keep his commandments" (Eccl 12:13). On Ellul's reading of Ecclesiastes, such "fear" involves respect, a stance of honest recognition and faithful submission rather than cowering intimidation in the face of arbitrary power. Proper fear of God has two inseparable dimensions: listening to God's word, and obeying God's commandments. Listening to God entails being receptive to divine revelation expressed in God's word, which confounds all human words. Obedience is the basis for being "free and intelligent, as you cease your madness and your vain questions," and "enables us both to live and to understand."[92] Taking these dimensions together, Ellul reaches a radically theocentric account of human life. Human wholeness or completeness, and human meaning, are found nowhere else and in nothing humanly created. Ellul concludes: "The thing that gives us existence, truth, and reality, the thing that suddenly creates us, is our relationship with God. This relationship constitutes the whole person, since stripping him of it leaves him with nothing else: we found that everything else was vanity."[93]

Apocalypse

Ellul's full-length (three-hundred-page) treatment of the book of Revelation, the last book in the Bible, appeared in French in 1975 and was translated into English in 1977. The French title is quite significant: *L'Apocalypse: Architecture en mouvement*, with the subtitle meaning "Architecture in Movement." For our purposes in this chapter, we will limit our focus to

---

91. Ellul, *Reason for Being*, 31.
92. Ibid., 295.
93. Ibid., 296.

Ellul's hermeneutical approach to Revelation. Space does not allow us to examine his specific exegetical claims about particular passages in the book; in any case, those claims are less important than his posture toward the book as a whole.

Not surprisingly, Ellul is critical of most interpreters of Revelation, whom he accuses of being guilty of focusing far too much on the details of the "trees" while failing to grasp the "forest" at all.[94] He insists that "the Apocalypse cannot be understood verse by verse" but "must be read as a whole."[95] In particular, too much focus on individual verses prevents a reader from appreciating the "movement" of the text: "The problem is less that of comprehending a section of the book than the movement which effects passage from one section to another. . . . It is necessary to restore this movement: the Apocalypse is not an immobile and definitive architectural whole, but it is in itself movement, which goes from a beginning to an end."[96] For him, Revelation is "propelled by an internal movement and the attempt must be made to recover this movement," but he warns that he is approaching that task "outside the scientific, exegetical method."[97]

Here we see Ellul rejecting what he considers to be some central conventions of mainstream "scientific" biblical scholarship in favor of what he calls a "naïve" reading of the text.[98] Spelling out his method, Ellul says that he does not seek to "produce a scientific work enumerating the multiple interpretations of each passage, confronting the arguments, or again working on a purely historical or structural reading."[99] Yet he adds immediately: "I do not abandon the search for a meaning." It is important to notice that Ellul explicitly affirms the existence of an author's "intentional meaning" in writing this text.[100] On Ellul's approach, the "Apocalypse of John is a text carefully constructed in function of a complex and unique message," and therefore the interpreter's chief task is "discerning both this unique structure and at the same time the meaning to which this totality refers."[101] Therefore, the author (whom Ellul understands to be the Apostle John)

---

94. Ellul, *Apocalypse*, 12.
95. Ibid.
96. Ibid.
97. Ibid.
98. Ibid.
99. Ibid., 11.
100. Ibid., 15.
101. Ellul, *Apocalypse*, 14.

desires "to convey meaning by the construction itself, by the organization, by the plan and structure of his work."[102] According to Ellul, and as with his position on Ecclesiastes, the text's meaning is located in "the relationship of part to part, in their connection, their progression," which is deciphered when the final state of the text is examined as a whole, not broken into small pieces. He finds that knowledge of the cultural milieu of the ancient text can be overstated by biblical scholars; he finds that such "historical exegetical research is certainly not useless, but it illuminates the meaning very little."[103] His overarching concern is that most professional exegetes "do not take account of what the book that they study claims to be. They reduce it to their categories."[104]

Rather, as we would expect from someone operating from the standpoint of "theological exegesis" or "theological interpretation of Scripture," Ellul insists that the book of Revelation is "a theological book" that "speaks of God, of the Action of God, and of his interaction with the creation" rather than having politics, piety, consolation, or forecasts as its central theme.[105] For Ellul, the Apocalypse is "a book in relation to Jesus Christ" whose theological theme is "the revelation that Jesus Christ is master of history; it does not at all contrast a bad present with a good future; it reveals the *present* work of God, it shows the *present* victory of Jesus Christ."[106] For that reason, he asserts with confidence the propriety of treating Revelation as a "theological book."[107] Indeed, Ellul's interpretation displays a deeply sophisticated theological vision found in Revelation.

In order to establish the validity of his approach, Ellul devotes the first chapter of his treatment to structural analysis, tracing the "movement" and "texture" of the book. His central argument is that the book itself is composed symmetrically in five parts, which are arranged around a "central axis, the center, by relation to which all the rest is organized." The five parts can be outlined as follows:

1. Chapters 2–4, The Word of the Lord to His Church;

2. Chapters 5–7, The History of Humanity on Earth;

---

102. Ibid., 15.
103. Ibid., 18.
104. Ibid., 29.
105. Ibid., 29.
106. Ibid., 31. Italics in original.
107. Ibid., 33.

3. Chapters 8–14:5, The Incarnation, Death and Resurrection of Jesus Christ;
4. Chapter 14:6–18, The Last Judgments;
5. Chapters 19–22:5, The New Creation, New Jerusalem, Kingdom of God.[108]

The "axis" is the incarnation and crucifixion of Jesus Christ, which Ellul locates as the main point of Revelation 11 and 12. Around this central part, there is a careful symmetry between the first part of the book (dealing with the church) and the fifth part of the book (describing the new creation). The second part (history) corresponds to the fourth part (which depicts "the judgment and the destruction of evil and of the powers").[109] In addition, in each of the five parts there is a vision of Jesus Christ.[110] Ellul comments: "There are five themes, each one coordinated to the others, tied together by an essential relationship, but not a progression either causal or historical."[111] What sort of relationship is it? Ellul argues that "the Apocalypse is not an incoherent series of repeated visions, nor a successive series, but a fundamentally dialectical movement."[112] The five parts of the "architecture in movement" reveal a "dialectical process" that is built into the book's organization. Ellul goes so far as to suggest that "practically every section" of Revelation has a dialectical structure.[113]

The dialectical structure reveals a dialectical message about what Fasching calls "the intersection of time with the Eternal."[114] According to Ellul:

> The Apocalypse does not describe a moment of history but reveals for us the permanent depth of the historical: it is then . . . a discernment of the Eternal in Time, of the action of the End in the Present, the discovery of the New Eon, not at the end of time, but in the present history, the Kingdom of God hidden in this world. It reveals, then, on the one hand, the core of the problem, the insoluble core, and does not just summon to passivity but to the specific work of hope. It reveals to us, on the other hand, the actual presence of the end, with its two possible meanings: it shows the

---

108. See also Fasching, *Thought of Jacques Ellul*, 72.
109. Ellul, *Apocalypse*, 50.
110. Ibid., 100.
111. Ibid., 50.
112. Ibid., 52.
113. Ibid., 53.
114. Fasching, *Thought of Jacques Ellul*, 71.

> *telos*, that is to say, the goal, which is here, and the conclusion, the limit which is included in history.[115]

A key word here is Ellul's reference to hope, which is a major theme of his discussion of Revelation and the complex interplay of human freedom and God's action in history. Ellul believes that "human hope" is what most interpreters "inflict" upon the book of Revelation: "all is going badly now, but, be reassured, all will go well tomorrow."[116] He utterly rejects this as the vision of the Apocalypse. He also rejects the reduction of authentic Christian hope to a theological confession, an abstract truth of faith. Rather, he offers an account of hope (influenced strongly by Kierkegaard) wherein Christian hope is lived reality, a way of life, an "affirmation of the 'in spite of'" and an "absurd affirmation of the reality of the resurrection" which is a "total risk."[117] This sort of hope is not merely possible for Christians, but essentially required, in virtue of the revelation of human history shown by the Apocalypse. For Ellul, in a daring exegetical move, the famous three horses—red, black, and pale—depicted in Rev 6:1–8 are understood to represent the "four chief components of history" so that "the history of men is made up of the intermingling of political power, economic power, forces of destruction, negation and death, and also of the Word of God."[118] These horsemen "are always the same" throughout every age; therefore, there is no "progress" and no "degeneration" in human history. Yet, in the midst of human history, the crucified Lamb, Jesus Christ, who is the Word of God, "discloses" these forces of history for what they are and reveals the meaning of human history as the realm of his presence and the domain of his paradoxical victory as the One who was dead and is risen, whose "victory will be comprehensible retrospectively only at the end."[119]

Conclusion

From our examination of Jacques Ellul's work as a biblical interpreter, it is clear that he was a careful and thorough, if sometimes idiosyncratic and daring, reader of Scripture. His extensive writings on Genesis 1–3 and his

---

115. Ellul, *Apocalypse*, 24. Italics in original.
116. Ibid., 55.
117. Ibid., 57.
118. Ibid., 150.
119. Ibid., 156.

book-length volumes on Jonah, Ecclesiastes, and Revelation are not "commentaries" in the conventional sense, but suggestive and provocative theologically oriented reflections on the Bible.

Three central features of his work as a biblical commentator mark Ellul as an unmistakable proponent of what is being called "theological interpretation" of Scripture. First, Ellul is entirely preoccupied with the meaning of the biblical text. His constant complaint is that typically exegetes focus on the historical context of the ancient world but do so without shedding much light on the author's intended meaning. Their narrowly historical interests prevent them from engaging theological content. In identifying the meaning of a text, Ellul's approach emphasizes tracing the logical flow of ideas by paying close attention to the literary features and organizational design of the book. For his work on both Ecclesiastes and Revelation, the decisive interpretive moves are prompted by nuanced observations about the literary structure of those books. It would be unfair to suggest that Ellul's approach to Scripture is undisciplined by the text itself or arbitrary in its interpretive decisions.

Second, Ellul's version of theological interpretation locates specific biblical passages or biblical books within a trajectory that typically marks out theological interpretation, which John Webster calls "the scope of the progress of the saving divine Word through time."[120] This approach is what Greg Allison has called the "message-theological" variation on theological interpretation, according to which a proper reading of the Bible shows "the predominance of the gospel of redemption wrought by God the Father through the life, sacrificial death, and resurrection of the Son of God, which good news is applied savingly by God the Holy Spirit and proclaimed in Scripture."[121] As a practitioner of this method, Ellul offers resolutely christological readings of both Old and New Testament texts. Clearly Ellul believes that Christ-centered readings must be given priority over all other theologically motivated readings of scripture (e.g., liberationist) and all other methodologies (e.g., historical-critical), while being free to draw insights from other approaches as it serves his purpose.

Finally, Ellul is a theological interpreter in the fundamental sense that he believes that Scripture is God's word for the church, that Christian seriousness involves an essential attentiveness to God's revelation in order to be equipped to play a distinctive role in the world, and that Christian

---

120. Webster, "Editorial," 116.
121. Allison, "Theological Interpretation of Scripture," 29.

scholarship that serves the church must be an interested, advocacy-minded scholarship that accentuates the Gospel of Jesus Christ.

CHAPTER 7

Ethics

"Freedom is not one element in the Christian life. . . . It is the Christian life."[1]

ELLUL'S ENTIRE CORPUS IS permeated with profound concerns about human character and conduct, about personal responsibility and freedom, and about resistance to dehumanization and depersonalization. Although Ellul's complete set of writings defy unqualified categorization, perhaps the most fitting way to describe him would be as a Christian ethicist, a thinker who seeks to explain how it is possible to live faithfully as a Christian under the cultural conditions created by the domination of technique. Although he wrote extensively in several areas of theology, Ellul stated that abstract theology "bores me immeasurably. . . . All these treatises on the nature of God do not interest me in the least. What is important to me is that which belongs to the ethical domain and the existential domain, in other words, what is close to life, to reality."[2] Indeed, Ellul wrote little doctrinal theology in the traditional sense, but a great deal about ethics. The overarching problem that absorbs Ellul's attention throughout his career is announced in the programmatic first chapter of *The Presence of the Kingdom*, namely, "The Christian in the World."

Careful readers of Ellul will find that he did what he said: "I refuse to construct a *system* of thought, or to offer up some Christian or prefabricated socio-political solutions. I want only to provide Christians with the means of thinking *for themselves* the meaning of their involvement in the

---
1. Ellul, *Ethics of Freedom*, 104.
2. Garrigou-Lagrange, *In Season*, 220.

modern world. Such is the essential goal of my work. It ends, necessarily, in a Christian ethics."[3] Ellul rejects many understandings of Christian ethics but believes that "an ethic needs to be formulated for the faithful so that they can truly be present to the world in which they live, and not to a past or unreal world. To achieve this formulation one must proceed first of all to a true and tangible acquaintance with this world and to a diagnosis of its condition. That cannot be done apart from ethical research."[4] The notion of being "present to the modern world" is at the heart of Ellul's work. Ellul's statement also reveals the central importance of ethics for Christian witness, and that his notion of cultural "diagnosis" necessarily involves moral reflection. For Ellul, social analysis always engages moral issues.

As we have repeatedly stressed, the most decisive influence on Ellul's theology was Karl Barth. This is also true of Ellul's approach to Christian ethics. While deeply indebted to Barth in many ways, for our purposes it is important to note that Ellul said that he discovered his "mission" from Barth. According to Ellul:

> I had the impression that the ethical consequences of Barth's theology had never been elicited. I was not satisfied from his volume of ethics and politics, which seemed to be based on an insufficient knowledge of the world and of politics. However, there was everything there necessary to formulate an ethic without losing any of the rediscovered truth, being totally faithful to the Scriptures, but without legalism or literalism.[5]

In this statement, Ellul affirms a fundamentally biblical approach to ethics. He aims to be "faithful to the Scriptures" in all his work. Frequent references to the Bible typify his way of addressing moral questions. Ellul's dissatisfaction with Barth helped focus Ellul's ethical work. For example, Ellul suggested that Barth was "guilty of confusion," naively lumping together "obedience to the state, service to the state, and participation in political life."[6] He also criticizes Barth for insufficient attention to the meaning of human freedom.[7] Thus, Barth's weakness was an inadequate cultural "diagnosis." The extent to which Ellul followed faithfully Barth's moral theology and the degree to which he blazed his own path as an ethical thinker is

3. Ibid., 6. Italics in original.
4. Ellul, *To Will and to Do*, 251.
5. Ellul, "Karl Barth and Us," 24.
6. Ellul, *Ethics of Freedom*, 370.
7. Ibid., 105.

a matter for future scholars to consider that is beyond the scope of our concern in this chapter.[8]

While most of Ellul's writings deal directly with moral concerns, this chapter will focus primarily on two major works that fall most clearly into the category of Christian ethics. The introductory volume to Ellul's intended four-volume series on ethics, *To Will and to Do*, appeared in English translation in 1969.[9] He intended to write more introductory material but appears to have abandoned that task.[10] Three substantive volumes were planned to work out the ethical implications of the theological virtues, because Ellul believed that "hope corresponds to an ethics of freedom, faith to an ethics of holiness, and love to an ethics of relationship."[11] Unfortunately, the series was never completed. Ellul's other chief ethical work is *The Ethics of Freedom*, published in English in 1976. It consists of the first volume and part of a third volume of his *Ethique de la liberté*, which appeared in 1973–74. The volume on the ethics of holiness is being prepared for posthumous publication by his son, Yves. The fourth volume, on the ethics of relationship, was never started.

The Christian Life as Agonistic Tension

Ellul's point of departure as a moral thinker is the inevitable experience of tension for the Christian in the world. For Ellul, authentic faith involves an "agonistic" way of life marked by wrestling, conflict, and opposition. Each Christian must wage "the fight of faith" as someone whose allegiance to Christ puts him or her deeply at odds with the world's ways. Drawing upon John's Gospel for a guiding image, Ellul asserts that "the Christian is necessarily *in* the world, but he is not *of* it. This means that his thought, his life, and his heart are not controlled by the world, and do not depend upon the world, for they belong to another Master."[12]

This starting point means that Ellul is acutely alert to the problems that arise from uncritical accommodation or compromise with the world's ways. But the Christian's task in the world is not to avoid compromise

---

8. See Bromiley, "Barth's Influence."

9. The book first appeared in French in 1964 with the title, *Le vouloir et le faire: Recherches éthiques pour les chrétiens*.

10. Ellul, *Ethics of Freedom*, 7.

11. Ibid.

12. Ellul, *Presence*, 2.

through passivity or disengagement. Withdrawal into a separate "closed group" or into a pietistic form of faith that is solely concerned with cultivating the "interior life" is unacceptable to Ellul. Rather, each Christian is to embrace his or her divine calling as someone "sent into this world by this Master," as someone with a "mission" in the world which involves fulfilling a specific "function" representing Christ and his kingdom.[13] Each Christian is to serve as a "sign" of God's covenant, God's grace, and God's action in the incarnation, death, and resurrection of Jesus Christ. Tension is unavoidable for someone living as a "sign" of Christ in the fallen world, which he calls "the domain of the Prince of this world, of Satan."[14] Ellul affirms a drastic "rupture" of the world through sin, with the result that "the world is in perpetual contradiction with the will of God."[15]

Ellul's most important contributions to Christian ethics revolve around his presentation of how Christians might live faithfully by maintaining the right sort of spiritual tension as "sent ones" who represent Christ in the world. But before discussing Ellul's positive account of Christian ethics, we need to recognize his insights into what he calls "technological morality," the ethical mindset that arises from the dominance of technique.

Morality in Technological Society

Profound moral unease lies at the heart of Ellul's critical evaluation of the modern world. Unabashed enthusiasm for technology and for technological "solutions" to human problems reflects society's movement in a disturbing moral direction. Ellul said that his scholarly motivation involved bringing to his audiences "an awareness of technological necessity and what it means . . . calling the sleeper to awake."[16] Modern people need to wake up to the dehumanizing and even "enslaving" implications of technique.

On his analysis, not only does the ascendency of technique involve the unchallenged accession to reductionist rationality, but so also does efficiency become the guiding social or even spiritual norm of an entire culture. Technique is not benignly amoral; technology is not neutral, as Ellul repeatedly shows. Instead, technique actually is an aggressively anti-moral factor in human society. Fueled by its own inner logic, technique

13. Ibid., 2–3.
14. Ibid.
15. Garrigou-Lagrange, *In Season*, 204.
16. Ellul, *Technological Society*, iii.

defies moral analysis. Says Ellul: "Technique never observes the distinction between moral and immoral use. It tends, on the contrary, to create a *completely independent technical morality*."[17]

Ellul offers a detailed exposition of "technological morality" as a way of thinking that "tends to bring human behavior into harmony with the technological world, to set up a new scale of values in terms of technology, and to create new virtues."[18] Technological morality establishes new standards for human behavior. The cultural dominance of technique and the ascendency of a technologically oriented society create the conditions for a very particular (and in Ellul's mind, very peculiar) moral way of thinking that is a troubling departure from all previous human history. In Ellul's terms, we have become its servant, whereby we enter into "subjection to technological values."[19]

Ellul identifies two "principal characteristics" of "technological morality." First, it focuses on "behavior" and is "solely interested in man's external conduct" (not intentions, ideals, etc.). What is deemed to be "good behavior is that which is called for by the technique, is described by the technique, is made possible by the technique."[20] Since technical progress is the supreme social value, "contemporary man is very generally convinced that the technique is the good, that it concurs in man's good and will bring about his happiness."[21] According to Ellul, technology and technical progress are not merely facts, or means, but are the standards by which we judge between right and wrong. Technique establishes "the criterion of good and evil. It gives meaning to life. It brings promise. It is the reason for acting and it demands our commitment."[22]

The second characteristic of "technological morality" is that this mindset becomes so pervasive and powerful that it "excludes moral questioning."[23] According to Ellul: "Man's decision is obtained through adhering to technical progress. There can be no debate, no personal decision

---

17. Ibid., 97. Italics added.
18. Ellul, *To Will and to Do*, 185.
19. Ibid., 187.
20. Ibid., 189.
21. Ibid.
22. Ibid., 190–91.
23. Ibid., 188.

involved in the matter. The good is obvious." He adds: "The technological good is irrefutable. It cannot be challenged."[24]

Ellul's examination continues by observing that "technological morality" sets up an unprecedented scale of values. First, technology itself is the decisive social value. "One can call everything in our society into question (including God), but not technology."[25] Second, "the normal tends to replace the moral. Man is no longer asked to act well, but to act normally."[26] The concept of the good increasingly is defined by what is commonly practiced. Ellul points to the famous, and now debunked, Kinsey Report (1948) on male sexuality as an example of how "it is no longer legitimate to declare good or evil that which is accepted as normal."[27] Ellul's point is that conduct that is "normal" in the sense of "statistically occurring regularly" is taken to be "normative" in the sense of carrying moral approval. Third, "good and evil are synonyms for success and failure."[28] In other words, what is ultimately normative is simply what works: "one does not argue with results."[29] This is the triumph of purely pragmatic moral criteria.

In addition to these new values, a new set of virtues is extolled that are all centered on the primacy of work for human life, especially technological work. Ellul pinpoints the centrality of virtues that are "all linked to the employment of techniques" that "really have as their aim to facilitate the working and utilization of techniques": "the virtues of self-control, of devotion, of trustworthiness in one's work, of responsibility in the performance of tasks, of loyalty, of sacrifice to one's occupation—all are fitted into the central cardinal virtue of 'doing good.'"[30] Ellul claims that other, more traditional moral virtues suffer a "gradual elimination": "family virtues, good fellowship, humor, play, etc."[31] Surely Ellul could have provided a stronger list of virtues, such as truthfulness, generosity, kindness, humility and others. He gives an example: "A man may act ignobly toward his comrades or his wife, but if he practices the virtues essential

---

24. Ellul, *To Will and to Do*, 190.
25. Ibid., 191.
26. Ibid., 192.
27. Ibid.
28. Ibid., 193.
29. Ibid., 194.
30. Ibid., 196.
31. Ibid.

to work all is forgiven him."[32] Ellul's point is that the "individual virtues of personal morality" are gradually eroded, while the collective virtues of technological efficiency are unquestioned.

Technological morality makes a virtue of unbridled "confidence in the future" that can be summed up in the slogan, "All is possible."[33] This is an ominous development for Ellul, as it "expresses a morality of the unbounded, of the limitless, to which modern man is perfectly adapted." He calls it "a morality of the gigantic" in which "man no longer recognizes any limits to his conquest."[34] The fundamental limits of human life are studiously ignored. Technical optimism is unbounded and unchallenged. A trenchant example of Ellul's worries about the advent of "a morality of the gigantic" and "the limitless" is the rise of a movement championing transhumanism; Ellul probably would agree with Francis Fukuyama that this is the "world's most dangerous idea."[35]

The Nature of Christian Ethics

Christians are to embrace an unavoidably uncomfortable position amidst technological society. Sent into that world on behalf of "another Master," they must not simply obey the impulses reinforced by technological morality. What guidance does Ellul offer to such people? For Ellul, living the "fight of faith" can be supported by the right sort of Christian ethic, but Ellul is wary of attempts to formulate "a complete and valid description of the demands of God."[36] He resists every effort to orient Christian ethics by "a series of rules, or principles, or slogans."[37] Rather, Christian ethics should be a "temporary" guide that is "continually revised, reexamined, and reshaped by the combined effort of the church as a whole," not an attempt at a "permanent solution to all problems."[38] Ellul is concerned that "the Christian ethic is not a means of resolving the Christian tension—that it is not a recipe for righteousness; that it is not a synthesis of the Christian faith and the world's values; that it is not a way of enabling the Christian to live

32. Ellul, *To Will and to Do*.
33. Ibid., 197.
34. Ibid.
35. Fukuyama, "Transhumanism." See also Fukuyama, *Our Posthuman Future*.
36. Ellul, *Presence*, 12.
37. Ibid.
38. Ibid., 14.

without the Holy Spirit."[39] Part of his approach involves rejecting the idea of natural law as well as the pursuit of a detailed moral casuistry, that is, case-based reasoning from general principles to specific applications covering a wide variety of life situations.

The theological basis for Ellul's constructive account of Christian ethics lies in its biblical grounding. On the first page of *To Will and to Do*, Ellul states emphatically:

> ... the criterion of my thoughts is the biblical revelation, the content of my thought is the biblical revelation, the point of departure is supplied by the biblical revelation, the method is the dialectic in accordance with which the biblical revelation is given to us, and the purpose is a search for the significance of the biblical revelation concerning ethics.[40]

The corresponding philosophical basis for Christian ethics, for which Ellul finds biblical evidence, is belief that "the good is the will of God." He explains: "It is not the good in itself that determines the will of God. It is the will of God which determines what is good, and there is no good which exists outside of that decision."[41] The underlying biblical rationale for Ellul's nominalism stems from his reading of Genesis 3. The primordial sin is the desire to be like God, knowing good and evil, which Ellul interprets to mean the impulse to discern or determine the material content of morality independently of God.[42] Once separated from God due to sin, human beings seek to define the good for themselves, despite being "radically incapable of discerning, loving, and willing God's good."[43] The good is only what God speaks in his word and must therefore be received through divine revelation. These factors prompt Ellul's conclusion that there is no natural moral knowledge and no intrinsic capacity to do God's will. On the contrary, "there is no possible knowledge of the good apart from a living and personal relationship with Jesus Christ."[44] This means that "morality" (as a merely human project, albeit well intended) is part of the world that belongs to the order of the fall and simply expresses human alienation from God. Even so, it has relative value in adding stability to human experience,

39. Ibid., 15.
40. Ellul, *To Will and to Do*, 1.
41. Ibid., 6.
42. Ibid., 13.
43. Ibid., 17.
44. Ibid., 16.

maintaining life and creation to some degree.[45] He affirms that "no society can exist and develop without a morality."[46] He warns Christians against treating natural morality as "useless," because it is indispensable to life in society. Yet it is inadequate for Christians. Ellul rejects natural morality on theological grounds. He states:

> In all the formulations of natural morality it is not a question of Jesus Christ. It is hard to see what purpose the work of God fulfilled in Jesus Christ can have in this construct. Neither the incarnation, nor the death, nor the resurrection have anything to do with the theory of natural morality. So one is confronted with a Christianity without Jesus Christ; for if man is able to compensate naturally for sin by his good conduct, if the fall is merely a "weakening," then there is in fact no need for Jesus Christ. Buddha, Socrates, or Nietzsche will do just as well for lifting man into moral or religious conformity with his nature.[47]

Methodologically, Ellul contends that any Christian pursuit of natural morality is mistaken because it involves "the transformation of the living event of love and grace into a principle of systematic construction, of elaboration and explanation. It is a utilization of the revelation for man's satisfaction, which has the effect of crystallizing and immobilizing that revelation in order to make it fit the system, thereby emptying it of all value."[48] The overall result is there is a "fundamental conflict between the inherent content of revelation and natural morality. For the church, the latter is always a way of conforming to the world."[49] That conformity is a denial of the proper tension that inevitably accompanies faithfulness to God.

Ellul's evaluation of the relative yet positive value of natural morality for non-Christians and for social order is an important part of his understanding of the role of Christians in the world. He asserts that "one of the essential rules of the Christian life is never to ask a non-Christian to conduct himself like a Christian."[50] This is the error of Constantianism, the "dreadful situation" that arises when a codified Christian moral standard is imposed on an entire population apart from confession of personal faith.

45. Ellul, *To Will and to Do*, 41.
46. Ibid., 159.
47. Ibid., 51–52.
48. Ibid., 52.
49. Ibid., 53.
50. Ibid., 104.

This transforms Christian morality into a universal morality, which eventually undercuts the vitality of Christianity itself.[51] For Ellul, the Christian should engage the moral issues of society primarily on the basis of society's own agreed moral standards, not on the basis of Christian revelation. Taking the example of Christian protests against state torture, Ellul contends that to protest "in the name of Jesus Christ is absurd. To protest in the name of the declaration of rights, a moral principle that the state itself has established, is legitimate. So the Christian, recognizing the relative validity of that morality, should recall it to non-Christians, for it is an element of the preservation of society, a principle of life; and he should, in a way, act as a guardian of it."[52] An important role for Christians in society is to hold the secular world accountable to its own best ideals and to work for its preservation.

But this is not the end of the story. For Ellul, the Christian is called not only to support the highest standards of secular morality, but also to speak publicly as a witness to the revealed will of God. Whenever "a Christian declares God's will in the presence of the state, then he introduces his own personal tension into society."[53] Interestingly, Ellul believes that Christians should introduce a healthy, dynamic tension into society through their verbal witness. He states: "When the Christian does not condemn, when instead of trying to do away with the world's morality he declares the consequences of the lordship of God, then he plays the most fruitful, the most positive, the most original role possible: putting the tension into society, and thus keeping it alive. He restores society's ability to develop. He offers a truly revolutionary interpretation of life. And it is precisely he alone who can play this role."[54] Ellul speaks of a "breach" in the wall of morality that human beings build for themselves, a "breach" through which God's word can pass when a Christian bears witnesses to a divinely revealed standard that contradicts the world's ways. When the word of God enters society in this way, there is "a judgment of that order by holiness. The explosion of the revelation destroys the ethic of the world."[55]

One of Ellul's contributions as an ethical thinker is his protest against "moralism." He writes, "God's revelation has nothing whatever to do with

51. Ellul, *To Will and to Do*, 101.
52. Ibid., 105–6.
53. Ibid., 107.
54. Ibid.
55. Ibid., 109.

morality. Nothing. Absolutely nothing."[56] He adds: "The Christian life is not a life conformed to a morality, but one conformed to a word revealed, present and living."[57] For Ellul, moralism is a failed attempt to resolve the proper tension that Christians should experience in the world through reliance on a man-made theory rather than a living relationship with God. He writes, "What makes a Christian out of a man is his confession that Christ is his Savior. Pagans can behave very well."[58] Ellul contends that neither the Hebrew Scriptures nor the New Testament present a detailed moral system to govern God's people in all times and places. His insight is that moralism eclipses the genuinely spiritual nature of Christian faith. Jesus called for a "radical change of being" through faith and criticized the Pharisees, who had "progressively substituted their own morality for the living and actual Word of God that can never be fixed in commandments."[59] Jesus "gives as his own commandment 'Follow me,' not a list of things to do or not to do. He shows us fully what it means to be a free person with no morality, but simply obeying the ever-new Word of God as it flashes forth."[60] Referring to the Apostle Paul's teaching on being "united with Christ," Ellul puts forward a stark opinion: "If we 'live in Christ,' as Paul puts it, there is no morality. If we observe morality, no life in Christ is possible."[61] At this point Ellul's readers might wonder if his rhetoric has not overstated the case. Taken in isolation, Ellul's attack on "morality" might sound alarmingly antinomian. It must be remembered that Ellul is opposing the reductionist supposition that conforming to a rigid, fixed code of moral laws is constitutive of Christianity. This supposition undermines the primary reality of Christian freedom, which is the central theme of his ethical thought.

The Ethics of Freedom

On one occasion Ellul remarked, "nothing I have done, experienced, or thought makes sense if it is not considered in the light of freedom."[62] Ellul made the ethics of freedom the first volume of his planned trilogy

56. Ellul, *To Will and to Do*, 69.
57. Ibid., 86.
58. Ibid., 75.
59. Ibid., 70.
60. Ibid.
61. Ellul, *Subversion*, 73.
62. Garrigou-Lagrange, *In Season*, 183.

"because I was increasingly convinced that freedom is the location and condition and arena of all Christian ethics and that holiness and relationship are possible only on the basis and in terms of the functioning of freedom."[63] In his fullest exposition of Christian ethics, he claims that "the most urgent and decisive task for Christianity today, on the basis of fellowship with Christ, is to recover the full meaning of freedom."[64] On this topic, Ellul does not hold back on criticism of the church. In his view, the fact that discussion on freedom has "vanished from the Christian horizon" is a major problem. "The believer is not concerned about knowing whether he is free nor is he worried in the least about ways of manifesting his freedom. In my view this is the very thing that explains the insipidity of the Christian life, its lack of meaning, its failure to make much impact on society."[65] He continues with a critique of conventional approaches to Christian ethics: "What is missing in all these works, in all these expressions of the Christian life, is the vital spring, the incontestable point, the incomprehensible quality, namely, freedom."[66] He concludes: "If there is no freedom there is no Christian life at all."[67]

Ellul's claim about the centrality of freedom for the Christian moral life has huge implications for his account of the nature of Christian ethics. He expounds a critical distinction between "ethics" and "morality" as follows:

> The importance of freedom as a condition of Christian ethics is so great that its presence or absence decides whether there is any Christian ethics or not. This alone constitutes the particularity of this ethics. The existence of the freedom of the Christian man is what makes it ethics rather than morality. If freedom is suppressed, then what is manifested as exhortation, the fruit of the Spirit, the free expression of grace, identity between the inner heart and the word that issues from it, the coherence of work and faith, the discovery of joy, is all turned back again into morality, into dull virtue, into a list, a decalogue, constraint, and the computation of merits.[68]

63. Ellul, *Ethics of Freedom*, 7.
64. Ibid., 193.
65. Ibid., 105.
66. Ibid., 105.
67. Ibid., 109.
68. Ibid., 111.

In this passage, we see Ellul's biblical theology at work, emphasizing what he takes to be the New Testament's own emphasis on grace and the work of the Spirit in giving guidance to Christians regarding their everyday life rather than teaching compliance with fixed rules.

An emphasis on the primacy of divine grace leads Ellul to contend that "ethics ought to flow out of the relationship with Christ."[69] This follows if freedom is defined by Christ's redeeming work. Freedom is not any sort of human ability or achievement or inherent quality, but rather is an unmerited gift of God: "Freedom is created by God for man and in man."[70] The work of Christ in redemption involves a change in being, not simply the demand of changed behavior. The metaphor of redemption when used to explain salvation by Christ assumes that human beings were originally free, and are restored to their proper freedom through Christ's intervention on the cross. Thus, "the freedom we have in Christ is a way of becoming new. Jesus Christ gives us a possibility of being which is quite different from any that we have in ourselves or can acquire by our own work."[71] Freedom comes from the outside, by a mediator acting to remedy our plight, but his action takes effect from the inside, at the level of being, not merely at the level of behavior.[72] A new mode of being is the result of Christ's redemption.

On this account, Christian freedom can easily slip back into a form of bondage in conformity to the world's ways. From this standpoint, we can see that Ellul is walking a fine line—Christians need guidance in living out their freedom, but the wrong sort of detailed guidance can destroy the entire project of freedom. In order to explicate how to live out this freedom, Ellul appeals to the temptation of Jesus in the wilderness as the paradigm of human freedom before God.[73] Facing severe pressure to compromise with the ways of the world, Jesus demonstrates that willing, voluntary obedience to God's word is the genuine nature of freedom. Ellul explains that the model of Jesus as the truly free person means that "freedom is not sitting back and letting God work. Freedom is knowing God's will and doing it."[74]

---

69. Ellul, *Ethics of Freedom*, 7.

70. Ibid., 13.

71. Ibid., 69.

72. Note the difference between the deep change effected by freedom in Christ and the superficial change, touching only behavior, effected by submission to technological morality.

73. See Matt 4:1–11; Luke 4:1–13.

74. Ellul, *Ethics of Freedom*, 62.

Jesus shows that "obedience to the will of God is freedom, and cannot be anything else."[75] This obedience is not "servitude" but service. There is an essential theological reason why: "If God himself is free . . . he surely cannot bear to be obeyed by slaves. He surely wants obedience to be free and voluntary, not out of fear and debasement. Love presupposes freedom."[76]

Obedience to God constitutes freedom. For Christians, as for Jesus in the temptation scene, human freedom will be expressed by hearing and obeying God's word in Scripture. "The only true, complete, absolute, and instrinsic freedom is the word of God. For this word is the basis and ground of our freedom, as it was of the freedom of Jesus himself."[77] This view has major consequences: "if our freedom comes from the word of God, this shows that it is mediated and indirect. It is not a nature that we may acquire. It is not direct apprehension. No matter what our pretensions may be, it is relative. It is never absolute in our lives nor do we accede to it absolutely. It is extrinsic. It is given us from outside. It comes as a new condition in which God has set us."[78] This approach demonstrates Ellul's affirmation of divine grace and the centrality of Scripture for the Christian life. Christian freedom is defined not only by Christ as Word of God, but by Scripture as word of God, since freedom involves "subjection to the word. It arises when men believe in the word, receive it, and bear witness to it. In so doing they are simply performing an act of obedience."[79]

A critical point for Ellul is that the Christian when redeemed by Christ is not put into a "state of freedom" and does not acquire a settled, habitual disposition of being free. Rather than a state, freedom is a capacity. Thus, "freedom is not a partial expression of the Christian life. It is not a fragment like joy or patience or faithfulness or temperance. Freedom, the freedom which God gives, is to be understood from the very first as a power or possibility. It is a power to act and to obey. It is a possibility of life and strength for combat."[80] The reference to "combat" recalls Ellul's foundational understanding of an "agonistic existence" of struggle and tension as the normal condition for Christians. For Ellul, the freedom of the Christian means being positioned to take, day by day, with fresh intention-

75. Ibid.
76. Ibid.
77. Ibid.
78. Ibid., 65.
79. Ibid.
80. Ibid., 103.

Ethics

ality in each situation, what we might call a determined "stance" of spiritual freedom, living out "a realignment and reorientation of life."[81] This involves what Ellul prefers to call "a way of life" or "mode of conduct" that is possible only for Christians. For him, freedom is "not a part or a fragmentary expression of the Christian life. It *is* the Christian life."[82]

Following Barth's lead, Ellul affirms that genuine freedom is always freedom for God and is always oriented toward service of God. The notion of freedom for God carries enormous moral weight. It entails that freedom "cannot be synonymous with emancipation, arbitrariness, or autonomy."[83] It is a freedom to recognize the authority of God, to become "responsible before God," seen as "a permission that has been given us and not a constraint, an authorization and not a duty."[84] This means obedience is not contradictory with freedom, despite what most non-Christians would think. At the same time, freedom for God means "liberation from self-centeredness" and from "being encumbered with the self, obsessed with the self, and enclosed in the self."[85] It also sets Christians free from "the powers," that is, the spiritual and institutional "forces which subjugate man" and serve as powerful "determinants" of human life.

Ellul is fond of citing the Apostle Paul's statements on freedom, including that for those with faith in Christ "all things are lawful" and "to the pure, all things are pure."[86] Ellul believes that Christian freedom is "alive, unlimited, without restrictions or obligations. It enables us to throw off all constraints and admonitions. It is true freedom: freedom to choose, to decide, to go where I want to go, to break that which dominates, to transgress prohibitions, to profane what man holds sacred, to conform if conformity is chosen and yet not to conform, to enter into and to break free from commitments, to give and to take back again."[87] Does this emphatic insistence on the complete freedom of the Christian mean a life without any moral limits? How can Ellul emphasize freedom so strongly without falling into the moral perils of subjectivism and relativism? Ellul himself asks whether

---

81. Ellul, *Ethics of Freedom*, 87.
82. Ibid., 104. Italics in original.
83. Ibid., 120.
84. Ibid., 122.
85. Ibid., 137.
86. See 1 Cor 6:12; 1 Cor 10:23; Titus 1:15.
87. Ellul, *Ethics of Freedom*, 186.

"adultery, eroticism, exploitation of the poor, and murder are things we may now do and God will not mind?"[88]

Ellul makes several key theological moves to prevent these errors. First, he stresses that the New Testament conception of freedom is *freedom in Christ,* which Ellul takes to mean that "the Holy Spirit dwells within us. I live, yet not I, but Christ lives in me. There has thus been a tremendous reversal which has changed the very root of our being and made us free. Hence, when we act, we no longer express the evil one; we express the Holy Spirit."[89] The Holy Spirit acts to bring a measure of moral restraint and orientation toward God, a point that Ellul could have developed further.

Second, Ellul argues that freedom "does not mean rejection of the law or revolt against God's order."[90] If freedom is for God, it will be expressed in ways consistent with God's revealed will. For Ellul, "the freedom which is given us is not the simple possibility of doing anything since nothing matters anyway. It is not an expression of the arbitrary and incoherent."[91] Ellul refers to Gal 5:13, which warns, "Use not liberty for an occasion to the flesh." He rejects the notion that "if all things are lawful," then "I can give free rein to my instincts, passions, and fantasies."[92] Freedom is not a "pretext for surrender to the passions."[93] Rather, it is a capacity to obey the will of God simply because it is the will of God and not because any of our independent faculties can justify the behavior.

Third, Ellul appeals to Augustine's famous dictum "Love [God] and do as you like."[94] The centrality of love then emerges in Ellul's approach. What does Ellul mean by love? Characteristically, he stresses that love must be spontaneous. Love of neighbor becomes a guiding moral norm, militating against both moral arbitrariness *and* the commonplace-as-norm ethics of technological morality. Ellul states: "Love by its very nature finds expression in the freedom to see and to choose what is good for others, what fits them best, what is in their interests. Love also means that nothing will be done to cause others to be grieved."[95] Genuine Christian freedom is other-

---

88. Ibid., 197.
89. Ibid., 188–89.
90. Ibid., 189.
91. Ibid., 198.
92. Ibid., 240.
93. Ibid., 243.
94. Ibid., 199.
95. Ibid., 201.

centered and cannot be self-indulgent. The importance of neighbor-love sets up a critical point: "love is not a restriction of freedom. It gives it its meaning and orientation. At the level of human behavior one might say that the totality of the Christian life amounts to a dialectic of freedom and love. Everything leads up to the movement in which freedom is incarnated in love and love stimulates freedom. The whole of ethics consists in this dialectical movement, constantly renewed, from love to freedom and from freedom to love."[96] Ellul offers a memorable analogy: "freedom without love resembles a blind man without a guide."[97]

The practical result of this dialectical understanding of freedom and love is that the Christian moral life involves freedom to be for God and for the neighbor, obeying the former and seeking the well-being of the latter, a commitment that is enacted in new ways in each situation. At times, Ellul seems to echo Joseph Fletcher's "situation ethics," as when he states:

> The Christian life cannot be ossified in a particular conception of the good. It must be a waiting and watching and praying and advancing. It must decide in each moment what is to be done. It must be ready to see who is the poorest and most deprived for whom everything must be done. It must also be ready to leave this one at once to go to someone else when there has been some relieving at least of his plight. In all this, of course, the rule of conduct is not to be our own imagination or desire or conformity or adaptation to changing society. It is to be only our assessment of the best possible expression of our love for the poor and the stranger and the enemy, i.e., for the neighbor.[98]

Ellul spells out the implication of this freedom to love one's neighbor through discreet, spontaneous acts of love: "The fact that freedom is a choice of acts in terms of love for others means that we are faced with a purely individualistic ethics. This freedom can be demonstrated only by individual acts in individual cases. Intrinsically and primarily it does not have any social or political dimension in the traditional sense."[99]

Finally, having put forth love for neighbor as a controlling moral norm, he adds a "second function" of Christian ethics: the glory of God. He

---

96. Ellul, *Ethics of Freedom*, 206.

97. Ibid., 207.

98. Ibid., 210. Ellul manages to avoid the antinomianism expressed by Joseph Fletcher in *Situation Ethics*.

99. Ellul, *Ethics of Freedom*, 210.

argues that "God's glory is his revelation, both general and particular, to the eyes of men."[100] Thus, when Scripture speaks of human beings glorifying God, "they really mean bearing witness to God. . . . It is a matter of showing him to those around us. It is a matter of acknowledging what God has done for us, of repenting and turning back to the life that God wills."[101] The result is that Christians are to exercise their freedom in Christ to make choices that maximize love for the neighbor—that advance their welfare, edify and build them up—and that glorify God, which means "to choose acts in which those who see them can find a reflection of God and learn thereby to love him."[102] There is an urgent matter of Christian "responsibility" since "only Christians can live it out and that if they fail there will be no freedom of any kind on earth. We have to assume it as the life which is accomplished for us. You are free and therefore be free; dare to be what basically and essentially you are."[103]

This imposing responsibility calls for ongoing acts of Christian "recognition," which has two salient features: first, "my task is to know and understand and scrutinize all that scripture has to say about this freedom which is now mine"; second, to recognize "alienation and unfreedom" in my situation, which he calls "a bitter business" in which we see how constrained and conditioned we are by external and social factors beyond our control and beyond our choice.[104] This is a perpetual challenge: "Recognizing our alienations is something that we have continually to begin again, to repeat, and to deepen. Hence freedom is always engagement."[105]

Those who study the Scriptures and their social context are then responsible for not falling back into bondage, forsaking their freedom in Christ. He says: "We can become slaves again. We can destroy freedom by not living it out."[106] Ellul catalogues some major ways of losing this freedom. He realizes the burden this places on the ordinary Christian layperson, saying, "The fact cannot be hidden that freedom is an exhausting business. Constantly to ask whether a decision or undertaking is to God's glory,

---

100. Ibid., 214.
101. Ibid., 215.
102. Ibid., 219.
103. Ibid., 223.
104. Ibid., 229, 230, 231.
105. Ibid., 234.
106. Ibid., 236.

whether it will edify the church or one's neighbors, is very tiring."[107] Ellul also warns against "following the social current," which results in what he calls "sociological bondage": "The fact that a man adopts without thinking the images, prejudices, and habits of his group, that he talks and judges and acts like the rest of its members, is bondage." This is "now accomplished by much more precise and rigorous means, by multiple techniques, by pedagogy, by public relations, by information, and by propaganda. All these are ways by which society enslaves man. Christian freedom has to defend itself against them, since they entail a basic attack on this freedom."[108] This calls for an active, alert vigilance. Failure of discernment regarding "sociological bondage" leads to disastrous consequences. In a stinging critique of the church, Ellul finds that "there is an extraordinary desire to be exactly like other men. We want no distinguishing marks. The Christian life is a good thing inwardly. Outwardly, however, we do as others do. We follow the dominant thrust of the age. We share the preoccupations, attitudes, and occupations of all the rest. The concerns and fads and allegiances and shifts of all are ours also. We do not speak boldly of a specific Christian morality or attitude. This would be to risk differentiation."[109] This is tragic for Ellul, since he sees the Christian's responsibility as being someone who can "undermine the pseudo-freedom of the structures and institutions of the world."[110]

Ellul is also very critical of the church's "refusal to aim at conversions." Making the glory of God a distinguishing mark of the Christian ethic involves an evangelistic dimension. He says, "We want to be present everywhere, to have a part in all human activities, to be businessmen with businessmen, royalists with royalists, intellectuals with intellectuals, trade union men with trade union men. This is all. We no longer talk of conversion. This would shock people. It would make us suspect. It would hamper our contacts. It would prevent us from being like others."[111] He continues:

> For what is the point of being present as Christians if it is not for the conversion of men? What is the unique aim of Christian action if it is not to lead men to acknowledge finally that Jesus Christ is their Saviour and Lord? Why is it that we join parties or unions or

107. Ellul, *Ethics of Freedom*, 238.
108. Ibid., 250.
109. Ibid., 254.
110. Ibid., 272.
111. Ibid., 254.

associations? Is it simply that we may have a part in movements that we regard as right in themselves? And are we to be bashful about telling others that we are acting as Christians? If we want to make Jesus Christ known, what does this mean? It cannot mean only imparting a vague and general knowledge, a kind of insubstantial presence. The aim must be that men confess Jesus Christ in heart and mouth. Anything else is an illusion. For Jesus Christ has not come to establish social justice any more than he has come to establish the power of the state or the reign of money or art. Jesus Christ has come to save men, and all that matters is that men may come to know him.[112]

Here Ellul echoes some contemporary theologians such as Hendrik Kraemer in emphasizing the critical role played by the Christian layperson.[113] "It is in the layman primarily that the powers, preoccupations, interests, and activities of the world meet the power of the Holy Spirit. It is in him that the determinations of the world meet freedom in Christ."[114] For Ellul, the church's role in society is focused almost entirely on the active, informed, faithful Christian layperson working out love of neighbor and witness to Christ in the midst of his or her various occupations. While not devaluing the importance of Christians in making the world more civil or livable, Ellul states: "Love and the glory of God do not have the task of helping the world to go its own way. The aim of Christian freedom is not that society should be better or should function better."[115] The layperson's evangelistic role is unrepeatable. This ministry "does not mean bringing non-Christians into the church but carrying the church to them."[116] He adds: "The church cannot continue to be a self-enclosed and self-incurved entity more or less tied up with sociological and class structures. On the other hand, taking the church to the world, which can be done only by laymen, has as its purpose the conversion to Jesus Christ of people who are reached in this way."[117]

What is the function of Christian ethics in preparing the layperson for this pivotal responsibility? Ellul writes:

---

112. Ibid., 254.

113. Ibid., 297. Ellul refers to the 1965 French edition of Kraemer, *Theology of the Laity*.

114. Ellul, *Ethics of Freedom*, 297.

115. Ibid., 299.

116. Ibid.

117. Ibid.

> We can never say: "This has to be done." For the hard-pressed layman who wants specific instructions there is no "Do this or that." There are no clear, simple, universal, Christian solutions to all the problems which arise. We can only put the problems as clearly as possible and then, having given the believer all the weapons that theology and piety can offer, say to him: "Now it is up to you to go and find the answer, not intellectually, but by living out your faith in this situation." There is no prefabricated solution or universally applicable model of Christian life. Freedom itself causes the difficulty. If we give orders, we deny freedom. If we deny freedom, it is of little value that Christians are present at a given place and act in a specific way, for they do indeed manifest themselves, but as true Christians. Freedom implies that each Christian discovers for himself the style and form of his action.[118]

This is a daunting picture of the spiritual and moral demands on the ordinary Christian life. Ellul provides some assistance by offering what might best be called an "activist spirituality of engagement." He explores the time-honored Christian theme of spiritual pilgrimage. To live out their faith in these ways, Christians need to become "strangers and pilgrims" who are "uprooted" in relation to material things and worldly attachments because "our witness has no validity if we are conformed to the world."[119] He calls upon Christians to "use" the world, with a clear sense of detachment from it, rather than "possessing" the world as other people do. This posture allows Christians to work for a "stable environment" for everyone, a "livable society," and to work at the "social level" against all forms of uprooting caused by political and economic misery, yet simultaneously to exercise freedom in relation to them, being able to stand apart and not invest themselves in such ventures unqualifiedly.

Ellul urges that this sort of fighting against "social" upheavals is "not by any means the summit of Christian action."[120] He speaks of the importance of "inner detachment" as they are engaged in worldly affairs. For instance, Ellul says that a Christian "might take part in politics, not because of a belief in the value of politics nor in the objectives to be attained . . . but purely because of the opportunity to meet men and to be present among them."[121] Christians "will systematically refuse to grant it the significance that others

---

118. Ibid., 300.
119. Ibid., 305.
120. Ibid., 308.
121. Ibid., 311.

do."[122] This is based on Ellul's core belief that Christian freedom means a "refusal of the central modern thesis that material change will bring about a change of life, being, and reality."[123] Rather, according to Ellul, it is only the gospel of Christ that can bring fundamental change at that level.

Unanswered Questions

This chapter has sketched Ellul's contributions in the realm of Christian ethics by analyzing his understanding of the Christian's distinctive role in the world, his assessment of the hazards of technological morality, his differentiation of "ethics" from "morality," his theology of the laity, and his nuanced theological account of Christian freedom. His assertively Protestant and largely Barthian christocentrism and biblicism have been demonstrated. On account of these insights, among others, Ellul's ethical writings deserve to be taken seriously and studied further by Christian laypeople as well as scholars.

Before closing, it is worth noting that Ellul's view of ethics leaves several important questions unanswered. Perhaps Ellul intended to address these issues in subsequent writings, and his forthcoming volume on the ethics of holiness might speak to them, but on the basis of what we have available at present, there are some noteworthy gaps. First, given Ellul's strong emphasis on the "agonistic" struggle of the Christian who bears weighty moral responsibility for the living out his or her freedom and who is meant to serve as a fearless, risk-taking, countercultural witness to Christ, we must ask: how does someone *become* the sort of person that Ellul envisions? How is such moral character developed? What methods of spiritual and moral development would Ellul advocate?

The ideal Christian as depicted in Ellul's ethical writings seems nothing less than a heroic figure—yet also a strangely solitary one. Ellul's approach to ethics hinges upon the capacity of the Christian to act wisely in any given situation, drawing upon a deep understanding of the Bible and a sophisticated analysis of his or her cultural context. But what sort of moral and spiritual formation is involved in becoming such a knowledgable, mature, and highly skilled person? In short, Ellul calls for transformed moral agents, but gives virtually no account of the process of moral transformation. Ellul's nearly exclusive focus upon the moment of action prevents

122. Ellul, *Ethics of Freedom*, 311.
123. Ibid., 319.

Ethics

him from giving an account of the shape of gradual preparation that would equip the Christian to live out his or her faith in the disciplined and creative ways he advocates. Ellul's inability to address this dimension of the moral life is linked to an underdeveloped account of the role of the Holy Spirit in Christian ethics.

A related question worth raising is: why are there are so few references to the Spirit in Ellul's nearly five-hundred-page *Ethics of Freedom*? A stronger biblical exposition of the Spirit's work in shaping Christian character, fostering Christian wisdom, and guiding Christian decisions would have strengthened Ellul's account of the moral life, would have been compatible with his overall theological vision, and might have been more faithful to the biblical witness to the freeing work of the Spirit.

Another unanswered question concerns his ecclesiology. Where is the gathered church in his understanding of the moral life? Ellul emphasizes the church's scattered life, as the people of God are dispersed across society throughout the week, sent out to provide a Christian presence in various arenas, making life livable in the "penultimate" realms of life while pointing people to "ultimate" ends of life found in Jesus Christ. His emphasis upon the laity's critical role in the world is commendable. Yet, he mentions only in passing that such laypeople are dependent upon the gathered Christian community for their development. A vibrant gathered church is logically necessary to accomplish his vision, yet where is an account of the church's corporate life? The overall picture so stresses the Christian in the world that Ellul has neglected the formative context of the Christian in the church, the fellowship of shared faith. Ellul's theology never develops a positive role of the corporate body of Christ, let alone any sense of the church's collective witness, even though he recognizes that "an indispensable condition for the layman if he is to carry the freedom which is given him and inscribe the incarnate presence of the Lord in decisions which do not conform to the schemata of society" is the church as "a strong body and community" that makes this witness "possible for the layman."[124] Ellul's constructive account of Christian ethics is hampered by an undeveloped understanding of the centrality of corporate worship, prayer, study, and fellowship as formative factors in moral development. These factors explain the rather exaggerated individualism of Ellul's viewpoint. Although Ellul described himself as a

---

124. Ibid., 298.

"man of friendships," his account of ethics reflects nothing of the importance of such relationships.[125]

Referring to Phil 4:14, "I have learned, in whatever state I am, therewith to be content," Ellul points out that being "content" is something that "Paul has learned . . . apprenticeship is required to be able to live in this freedom regarding honor or humiliation, riches or poverty." But this proves to be only a passing reference to apprenticeship. Surely the Apostle Paul was no solitary Christian. As a convert to Christ, he benefited from an intensive mentoring relationship with Barnabas, a respected elder in the Jerusalem church. Thus, the notion of apprenticeship (or mentoring) appears to be utterly critical to becoming the sort of person that Ellul envisions, but his writings lack discussion of any such connection. Ellul mentions few exemplars of the sort of authentic freedom he advocates, apart from Jesus. Readers of Ellul who are inspired by his vision of Christian freedom will need to supplement his writings with resources related to spiritual and moral formation if they are to exercise faithful presence in the modern world.

---

125. Garrigou-Lagrange, *In Season*, 23.

CHAPTER 8

Ellul as a Christian Scholar

"In truth, however, my attempt seems to have failed: no one is using my studies in correlation with one another, so as to get at the heart of our crisis in a conscious manner, based on a Christian understanding of it."[1]

READERS OF ELLUL OFTEN find the task before them to be daunting. Some of Ellul's most significant works, such as *The Technological Society*, are his most dense. Many of his works present readers with the challenge of apparent circularity; Ellul sometimes seems to complete a thought only to come back to it later for further elaboration or development in light of his intervening arguments. Those who keep at the task despite these challenges are rewarded with understanding the work of one of the most significant interpreters of the central challenges of the late twentieth century. Even those who are tempted to lash out at Ellul's provocations will find in Ellul's work a rewarding confrontation with a demanding thinker. Those who disagree with Ellul may discover that he helps them ask important new questions, though they differ with him on the answers. Moreover, even those who find that they do not fully understand Ellul often find that they understand other things better in light of Ellul. Ellul has something for everyone.

Yet Ellul presents a special challenge to those who take up more than one of his works. Readers who have successfully traversed the terrain of one work by Ellul often believe that they understand Ellul's assumptions, methods, and conclusions. However, those same readers are often confounded

1. Ellul, "On Dialectic," 307.

upon picking up another book in Ellul's corpus and encountering what seem to be very different assumptions, methods, and conclusions. The fact of the matter is that when one begins to read Ellul, understanding increases. Paradoxically, as one continues to read, understanding decreases for some time until, in fact, the average reader *misunderstands* Ellul. One must eventually read attentively a great number of pages of Ellul's writing before finally coming again to a clear understanding of Ellul's arguments. At this point, most readers are finally able to wrestle with Ellul's positions and their implications and to appropriate and employ Ellul's arguments in the study of issues to which Ellul himself did not apply his own approach. This relationship between reading volume and understanding is represented below in what we call the "Ellul Understanding Curve."

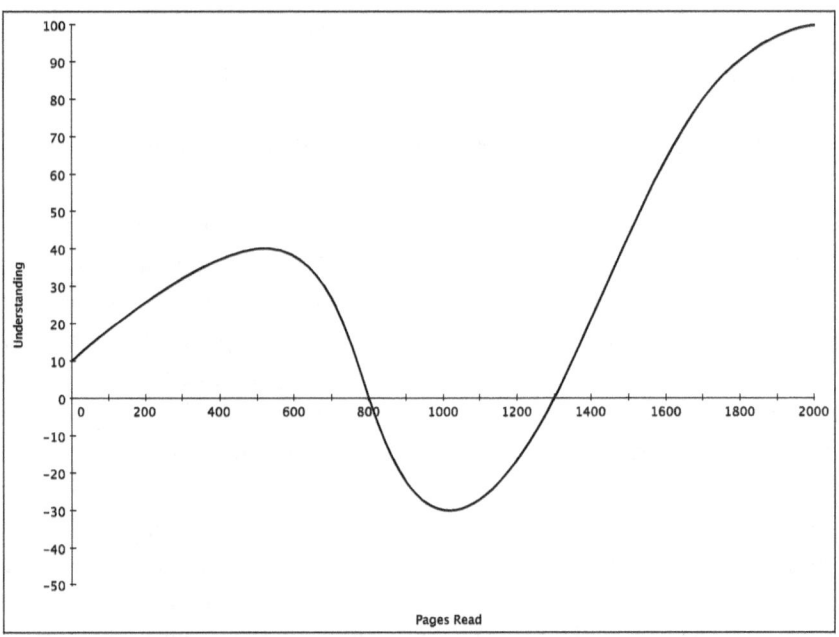

Figure 1. The Ellul Understanding Curve (numbers are only suggestive)

This tendency toward misunderstanding is a widely known feature of Ellul's work. David Menninger rightly commented: "Few social or political critics have been as misunderstood or underestimated as Jacques Ellul."[2] It is easy to take a given statement by Ellul out of context. It is also difficult to summarize his work succinctly or accurately. Most of his writing defies

2. Menninger, "Politics or Technique?," 110.

easy classification. The translator of Ellul's most famous work, *The Technological Society*, wrote that the book "is certain to be an enigma, and even a scandal, to many. It is not sociology, political economy, history, or any other academic discipline, at least as those terms are usually understood."[3] Most readers of Ellul's works are dependent upon English translations that can miss the nuance of his French original. In particular, a major factor that contributes to misunderstanding Ellul is that most scholars and students typically read only small portions of his overall body of work. Because he does not produce an integrated, synthetic, or systematic set of writings, those who are interested in his thought need to study quite a few of Ellul's books; the more one reads, the more the other works make sense.

In fairness to his readers, and without being uncharitable toward Ellul, the fact is that Ellul's style of writing tends to contribute to misapprehension. Reading Ellul takes patience. Many of his books tend to ramble repetitively and some offer labyrinthine treatments of complex subjects. His views are often idiosyncratic and are marked by strong assertions. Even the most enthusiastic of Ellul's followers will admit that he is prone to the typical hazards of prophetic writings, whether ancient or contemporary. David Gill affirms that Ellul is a "genius and a man of vast learning and erudition" yet is given to "habitual overstatement."[4] Gill suggests that Ellul "is highly persuasive in what he affirms, much less so in what he denies."[5] Gill explains that Ellul was "writing in the heat of passion and concern and engages in rhetorical exaggeration to try to provoke the degree of response that will ultimately redeem a situation."[6] In light of these difficulties with Ellul's writing style, John Wilkinson suggests that an interpreter of Ellul needs to "persuade sensible people" who are trying to read Ellul not to "throw down" one of his books "before they have negotiated even the first ten pages."[7] If this is true, the lack of understanding is a tragedy for the community of those who would read the scholar that Clifford Christians has called "the C. S. Lewis of the social sciences."[8]

---

3. Wilkinson, "Translator's Introduction," xii.
4. Gill, *Word of God in the Ethics of Jacques Ellul*, 183.
5. Ibid., 164.
6. Ibid., 183.
7. Wilkinson, "Introduction," xii.
8. Christians described Ellul this way in a visit to Wheaton College, in Wheaton, Illinois, in the fall of 2009. Lewis was an Anglican Oxford professor of literature and a significant contributor to Christian thinking in the twentieth century.

Understanding Jacques Ellul

One of Ellul's major translators, G. W. Bromiley, suggests: "If Ellul's work is to achieve its proper effect it should not be read as a definitive statement which one can appropriate only if assent is given but rather as a spur or stimulus which provokes new and exciting effort. Ellul may often be wrong but he is never platitudinous or dull. Much can be gained from his acute and informed expositions. Even more can be gained, however, from critical interaction with his original and brilliant discussions."[9] The key word in Bromiley's proposal is "critical." Similarly, Martin Marty contends that Ellul "does merit a readership that will confront and argue with him and his vision. . . . One engages the thought of Ellul; there is no such thing as a casual reading followed by mild acceptance or bland rejection."[10]

But if one has a strategy for understanding Ellul, engagement with Ellul's thought certainly is worth the effort. Ellul writes to provoke a reaction in his readers. His writings are a valuable stimulus for our own reflections, arguments, and decisions. The good news is that one begins by understanding more of Ellul than one knows and that by pushing through difficult texts, one can come to understand better not only Ellul but also the world in which we live. But what accounts for the challenges attendant to reading Ellul? What explains the dip in understanding? We propose that these are explained by three related issues:

1. Ellul worked in two arenas—social theory and theology—separated by a wide gulf due to secularization and specialization that have attended modern scholarship. While Ellul's body of work bridges this divide, for the most part, he kept these types of work separate, addressing each in separate books in which he wrote more or less according to the very different standards of each field. In his works of social theory, for example, he did not employ the methods of theology, but employed those assumptions and methods common to social theory. And in his works of theology, he did not employ the methods of social theory but employed the assumptions and methods common to theology. According to Ellul, there is a reason for his writing strategy:

> I have sought to confront theological and biblical knowledge and sociological analysis without trying to come to any artificial or philosophical analysis: instead I try to place the two face to face, in order to shed some light on what is real socially and real spiritually. That is why I can say that the reply to each of my sociological

9 Bromiley, "Editor's Preface," 5.
10. Marty, "Creative Misuses of Jacques Ellul," 3–4.

Ellul as a Christian Scholar

analyses is found implicitly in a corresponding theological book, and inversely, my theology is fed on socio-political experience. But I refuse to construct a *system* of thought, or to offer up some Christian or prefabricated socio-political solutions. I want only to provide Christians with the means of thinking out *for themselves* the meaning of their involvement in the modern world.[11]

So Ellul's readers encounter one type of work at a time and may find transitioning from one to the other to be difficult.

2. Relatedly, and just as importantly, despite the fact that Ellul's work in these two separate fields reflected assumptions and methods common to each, Ellul was a Christian scholar who never left his faith behind, no matter what he was working on, even if it was a topic in social theory. He allowed biblical and theological understanding to interrogate and to critique the full range of social theoretical work. Whether he was engaging social theory from the standpoint of theology—as he does in *The Politics of God and the Politics of Man*—or relying upon theological insights in a work of social theory—as he does in *The Humiliation of the Word*—he always allowed his Christian faith to permeate his work. This is evident even in what Ellul does *not* write in a given book. Ellul's most "secular" work—*The Technological Society*—was also his most popular, provocative, and, for some of his readers, frustrating. It is Ellul at his most seemingly deterministic and pessimistic, in part because he refuses to offer false hope of escape from the "challenge of the century." Instead, Ellul writes in the preface to the work that, perhaps if we pray, God will deliver us from our technical prepossessions. He then goes on for over four hundred pages to describe a situation for which he offers no human solution. Ellul indirectly invokes God even in what he does *not* say, by espousing no other hope. In this way, much of his sociological work can be framed by the epigraph he chose for the section on vanity in *The Reason for Being*, his commentary on Ecclesiastes: "In order to be prepared to hope in what does not deceive, we must first lose hope in everything that deceives."[12]

3. Third, Ellul expected and, indeed, hoped that his corpus would be read and understood as a whole, that his readers—whether or not they

---

11. "From Jacques Ellul," 6. Italics in original.
12. Georges Bernano, cited in Jacques Ellul, *Reason for Being*, 47.

themselves were Christians—would not divorce his theological work from his social theory any more than he did, even though the two did appear in different texts. As Ellul himself notes, "I have not actually written a wide variety of books, but rather one long book in which each 'individual book' constitutes a chapter. It's a gamble and a little insane to believe that there will be some readers patient enough to see how my . . . works hang together."[13] The epigraph for this chapter appears in an essay that Jacques Ellul wrote as an epilogue to a collection of papers interpreting his work. Its sternness gives us pause as authors who attempt to interpret Ellul and to make sense of his work by weaving together the threads of Ellul's ideas for a readership that will have limited exposure of its own. No one, Ellul felt, was reading his work the way he meant for it to be read. Everyone was encountering Ellul, but no one, it seems, was encountering Ellul on his own terms.

What would it mean to encounter Ellul on his own terms? What would it mean to read Ellul the way he meant himself to be read? What would it mean to use his studies "in correlation with one another"? In order to properly understand any aspect of Ellul's work, one must understand both parts of his work *and* the relationship between them. Ultimately, this is the reason for the Ellul Understanding Curve. In order to fully understand Ellul, one must read sufficiently across both his theological and social theoretical work *and* one must learn how Ellul related one to the other. In closing our introduction to Ellul, it is worth examining Ellul's distinctive mode of integrating faith and learning, as well as his integration of scholarship and practice, in an effort to understand better his life and his work.

Ellul's Modes of Integration: Correlation, Questions, Dialectic

Ellul was trained in law—which is not to say that he was trained in the practice of law. In France at the time of Ellul's studies, training in law involved the study of the history of social and political institutions (thus Ellul's still untranslated early work on the history of institutions). Few courses of study could have fit Ellul more for a career of studying the social origins and implications of political, social, and technical novelties and the patterns of

---

13. Ellul, *Ellul on Religion, Technology, and Politics*, 22.

stability and dynamism that govern these phenomena. Professionally, Ellul was a social theorist.

At the same time, Ellul was an amateur theologian. This term is not necessarily a criticism of the quality of his work, but is more a comment about the extent of his training. He did complete a full course of seminary studies, but never received a theological degree. Throughout his life, Ellul was an "amateur theologian" in the best and most literal sense of the word—a genuine lover of the Bible and of theology. He refused to allow his status as an "outsider" in theological circles to prevent him from engaging in ambitious and sophisticated Christian reflection. Rather, his "outsider" status gave a freshness and vibrancy to his theologizing that all too often is missing in the writings of "professionals" in the field. All of Ellul's work proceeded from "faith seeking understanding," to use Anselm's definition of the task of theology. His writings reflect an impressive breadth of biblical knowledge and a vigorous engagement with assumptions and methods of mainstream professional theologians of his time. Clearly Ellul's work in theology was important to how he thought about issues of social theory.

But how did Ellul relate these two tasks: that of the professionally trained social theorist and that of the amateur theologian? In order to understand Ellul's work as a Christian scholar, one must understand the concepts of correlation, the necessity of well-formulated questions and problems, and a dialectical approach to answering those questions.

Correlation

What Ellul lamented was that no one was reading his work as a social theorist alongside his theological work. He is, however, very specific about the way in which he had hoped that these two would be read together. He notes that his readers were *not encountering his work in correlation.*

Ellul did see a relationship between his sociological writings and his theological writings as a dialectical one: "It is not possible to read the one without the other."[14] Ellul said that "the sum of [his] books constitutes a whole consciously conceived as such."[15] This "whole" should be conceived in light of what Ellul called "a correspondence between apparently unrelated books." For example, he noted the relationship between *The Political Illusion* and *The Politics of God and the Politics of Man* and indicated that *The*

14. Ibid., 90.
15. Ellul, "On Dialectic," 304.

Ethics of Freedom was "the exact dialectical counterpart of the two books on technology (*The Technological Society* and *The Technical System*)."[16]

Looking at Ellul's body of work, it is clear that there are pairs or clusters of volumes that constitute distinctive constellations within the universe of Ellul's work: for example, *The Technological Society*, *The Technological Bluff*, *The Technological System*. Within these constellations, however, there is often a visible divide between the work of Ellul, social theorist, and the work of Ellul, amateur theologian—the same divide that characterizes his whole corpus: for example, *The Political Illusion* and *The Politics of God and the Politics of Man*. While Ellul does not mean for these to be read with a codebreaker's mindset and an Enigma machine, he wants his readers to encounter his works in "correlation." But what does a pattern of correlation look like in Ellul's work?

In order to understand this concept, it would perhaps be instructive to compare Ellul's approach to that of theologian Paul Tillich, one of the giants of twentieth-century theology. In volume 1 of his *Systematic Theology*, Tillich writes, "Systematic theology uses the method of correlation. It has always done so, sometimes more, sometimes less, consciously, and must do so consciously and outspokenly, especially if the apologetic point of view is to prevail. The method of correlation explains the contents of the Christian faith through existential questions and theological answers in mutual interdependence."[17] Like Tillich's method of correlation, Ellul often explained the contents of the Christian faith by identifying theological answers to troubling and existentially challenging questions. To be sure, though, there are profound and important differences between Ellul's approach and Tillich's. The most significant of these emerge from Ellul's commitment to a more or less neoorthodox, and specifically Barthian, analysis. Ellul, like Barth, could not have embraced "mutual interdependence" between God and human beings in the same way that Tillich did.[18] Likewise, Ellul was not preoccupied with what Tillich referred to as existential questions.[19] Nor would Ellul have turned for theological answers strictly to Christian *symbols*.

---

16. Ibid., 306.

17. Paul Tillich, *Systematic Theology*, 1:60.

18. Ibid., 61.

19. Nevetheless, given Ellul's affinity for Kierkegaard, we should not be surprised at Ellul's affinity for the same types of questions and approaches that motivate thinkers who are concerned with existential problems.

However, where Tillich specifies the role of correlation in the "cognitive side" of the "divine-human relationship," there is significant overlap between Tillich's elaboration of correlation and Ellul's own approach. As Tillich writes, "God answers man's questions, and under the impact of God's answers man asks them. Theology formulates the questions implied in human existence, and theology formulates the answers implied in divine self-manifestation under the guidance implied in human existence."[20] We may think of Ellul's work in this way: Ellul formulates questions implied in contemporary human existence, especially those questions pertaining to or emerging from shifting patterns of social interaction. He then formulates the answers implied by divine revelation.

Specifically, Ellul correlates what he called "truth" and what he called "reality," which were one before the fall and curse and will again be one in the new creation. In the meantime, there is a rupture between truth—the way things ought to be—and reality—the way things are. The job of the Christian is to bring the answers and solutions of truth to bear upon the questions and problems of reality—to "maintain a breach" in reality through which truth can be seen.

This pattern can be seen in Ellul's work on politics, for example. In *The Political Illusion*, he formulates the questions implied by political realities, but he offers no interpretation of the source of the problem, no positive response, and no solution from within political thought or practice. Rather, in order to understand both the problem and the solution, he turns to divine revelation as offered in the book of 2 Kings, which he presents in *The Politics of God and the Politics of Man*. For Ellul, hope is the place where the two sides of his correlative work meet. His social theoretical work offers no genuine hope, creating a crisis for the reader, while his theological work offers the hope of God's new creation.[21]

Questions

For Ellul, the power of this correlative approach was located in our capacities to ask the right questions. In his essay "Needed: A New Karl Marx!"—the second in a series on the "Problems of Civilization"—Ellul writes,

---

20. Tillich, *Systematic Theology*, 1:61.
21. Ellul, *Ellul on Religion, Technology, and Politics*, 22.

> This is the folly of our time: we claim to give solutions without even looking at the problems. We cast a superficial glance over the world and pretend to organize it for a thousand years. It is not one of the least contradictory traits of our epoch that we demand answers before we are capable of formulating clearly the questions . . . Solutions to what? That is one of the most suggestive surprises there might be. . . . Nobody is concerned to know the problem. One begins with the very general and vague idea: "it's not working." What? Everything: the economic, the political, and social. More precisely? Unimportant. Vain analyses, mind games. What is needed is a remedy, and that right away. . . . Now these problems are all, without exception, wrongly posed because they are conceived as causes when they are only effects. . . . The problem is posed well enough in reality, in the practical life, but it is not formulated, it is not intellectually, analytically conceived. Now it is impossible to answer a question when the question is not thus posed.[22]

For Ellul, it is not enough to consider and treat our symptoms; our analysis must penetrate to the depths of our problems. We must not rush to answers before properly formulating our questions. Elsewhere, he writes,

> We tie ourselves to exterior forms without searching for their deeper reality. We want to combat social injustice, and that is very good, and we connect it to an economic system, but we do not penetrate the true structures of this system. We do not attempt to penetrate into the lair of the blacksmith who is forging our chains, whether because of a sacred fear of this mystery or because of an incapacity to go far enough. . . . Nevertheless, it is only by going beyond that that we will have any chance of encountering the more stable reality on which the shifting problems depend. It is in such a descent into hell that we might be able to grasp the element of continuity according to which the current difficulties are propelled. It is in attacking these roots that we have a chance of reaching the tree itself, and not in the chasing of leaves blown by the hazards of the wind.[23]

Ellul's approach to formulating questions that can only be answered at the intersection of faith and learning included two steps:

---

22. Ellul, "New Karl Marx," 36–37.
23. Ellul, "By Way of a Brief Preface," 14.

Ellul as a Christian Scholar

1. Ask questions about a topic until the heart of the matter is discovered. Do not stop asking questions about the topic until the foundations of the matter are reached and no further questions can be asked without turning outside of the subject matter at hand for answers. Whatever one does, one should not presume to offer answers to the question or solutions to the problem from within the problem set itself. That is, if one finally arrives at the existential and spiritual heart of the political or technological problem, one will not find the solution to this problem within the realm of politics or technology. This step is most obviously taken in Ellul's non-theological works, like *The Technological Society*. Sometimes, though, it is implicit or embedded in Ellul's theological work.

2. In completing the first step, Ellul usually arrived at the conclusion that there was no human solution. Indeed, once the spiritual heart of the matter is discovered, there was for Ellul but one place to turn for spiritual answers: God's self-revelation in Scripture. For Ellul, this is the only way to arrive at true solutions to our problems. Here the influence of Barth upon Ellul's rejection of natural law is important. Like Barth, Ellul regarded with suspicion solutions that might emerge from the world of human activity, suggesting that the fall and the curse have so corrupted the world as to entirely disqualify it from offering any solutions whatsoever. Also like Barth, Ellul regarded the word of God as the only source of possible solutions to the problems of human beings. Any true progress would come only from God's initiative toward creation and through his self-revelation. So for Ellul, the second step was to examine the answers given in Scripture.

Indeed, Ellul describes his work in precisely this way during a conversation with Patrick Troude-Chastenet:

> Chastenet: "You seem happy to play on two registers: The theological and the socio-political. In your works, we find the same kind of analysis, adapted to different fields of study. This is the case, for example, with *Politique de dieu, politique des homes* [*Politics of God, Politics of Man*] and *L'Illusion Politique*, published one year earlier. Is it possible to consider one aspect of your work without having to refer to the other?"
>
> Ellul: "If you were to look at one without the other there would always be something missing. If you only take the theological dimension into account, you miss the element of incarnation. If

you restrict yourself to looking at the socio-political dimension, you will be constantly running up against a lack of answers and narrowness."[24]

The correlation of question—accessible according to Ellul by what he and Troude-Chastenet call "socio-political" study—and answer—accessible through theological inquiry—is indeed at the heart of Ellul's approach.

Dialectic

How, exactly, does Ellul go about the process of working with these questions and answers? In "On Dialectic," he writes that he found it impossible "to make a unity of the study of modern society" and "equally impossible to do a theological study without reference to the world," so that he had to find a relationship between the two, "and this could only be the dialectical process."[25] Ellul once said: "I am a dialectician above all; I believe nothing can be understood without dialectical analysis."[26] For this reason, Daniel Clendenin suggests that "dialectic is the kernel, the operative assumption which underlies all he has written. Those for whom dialectic is a stumbling block or a rock of offence will never appreciate or understand Ellul."[27]

The most important element is, for Ellul, that "dialectic is a procedure that does not exclude contraries, but includes them."[28] He compared their relationship to "the same way as a negative pole and a positive pole interact and then sparks fly between them."[29] According to Ellul, dialectic is "not just a way of reasoning by question and answer but an intellectual mode of grasping the real, which itself embraces both the positive and the negative, both white and black."[30] On his approach, "the real embraces . . . contradictory factors which do not cancel one another but coexist."[31] He

---

24. Ellul, *Ellul on Religion, Technology, and Politics*, 21–22.
25. Ellul, "On Dialectic," 305.
26. Ellul, "Interviews with Jacques Ellul," 224.
27. Clendenin, *Theological Method in Jacques Ellul*, 29.
28. Ellul, *Perspectives*, 7.
29. Ellul, *Ellul on Religion, Technology, and Politics*, 91.
30. Ellul, "On Dialectic," 293.
31. Ibid.

adds that thinking dialectically is an alternative to thinking in strictly linear categories or exclusively in terms of "either-or's."[32]

Although Ellul encountered the concept of dialectic through the writings of Karl Marx, he nevertheless insisted that "Christianity and biblical thought are dialectical."[33] In fact, he argues that in the Old Testament, "the Hebrews formulated God's revelation dialectically."[34] In fact, he asserts that scriptural revelation itself is "fundamentally and intrinsically dialectical."[35] One of his favorite examples of dialectic is the statement by the Apostle Paul, "You are saved by grace; therefore work out your salvation with fear and trembling," which Ellul calls "an obvious contradiction" because "if we are saved by grace there is no need to work out our salvation and vice versa."[36] Ellul insists that this dialectical tension is irreducible. He explains: "This is dialectical thinking: once you are saved, you are integrated into history, into a process leading to your salvation, which is given to you in advance, but which you have to implement, which you have to achieve, which you have to somehow take in hand and utilize. But this cannot be done on an intellectual and schematic level. It will be done in the course of your life. That is why we are dealing with something contradictory, yet it is not contradictory when we live it . . . in the process of life, this is perfectly resolved."[37]

For Ellul, the answer that God gives to social problems is always no and yes. That is, Ellul regards God's responses to our problems as both condemning and redeeming. As we have observed in our chapter on *The Meaning of the City*, Ellul believes that God's work in the world both condemns the work of humankind and promises to redeem that same work. This is, for Ellul, the theological dimension of dialectic, which "is a matter of entering a new phase in which the two contradictory statements are adopted and make progress possible."[38]

Without this act of God in human history, all would be lost. Ellul, and not just his readers, would be hopeless: "Without God, my work would have an eminently tragic meaning. It would have driven me to. . . suicide. I

32. Ibid., 299.
33. Garrigou-Lagrange, *In Season*, 202.
34. Elul, "On Dialectic," 298.
35. Ibid., 304.
36. Ibid., 302.
37. Ellul, *Perspectives*, 9.
38. Ellul, "On Dialectic," 292.

describe a world with no prospects but I have the conviction that God accompanies man throughout history."³⁹ For Ellul, the fragility, turmoil, and despair of history is met by stability, reconciliation, and hope from beyond time. God, through judgment *and* adoption in the work of Jesus Christ, both negates *and* affirms his creatures and their work. This is a dialectic of profoundest importance.

Praxis

Ellul's Christian scholarship did not limit him to the ivory tower. His work was not strictly in lecture halls and archives. While Ellul's recommendations for action were sometimes oblique and abstract to a fault, we can learn something from the way that he was involved in the affairs of his times. Ellul was heavily involved in local and national movements, serving as a lay pastor and bible study teacher and as a leader of the movement to save the Aquitaine coast from pollution. He was for a time a public servant in Bourdeaux. After a period of service in municipal government, he abandoned politics, but he never abandoned the project of coupling reflection and action. As Patrick Troude-Chastenet writes,⁴⁰

> From the early post-war period Jacques Ellul held a position of national responsibility at the head of the Reformed Church, which did not prevent him from remaining marginal within the Protestant community, often he was better thought of by Jews and Catholics than by his co-religionists. His involvement in the present age fueled his writing. He rekindled the tradition of camps in the mountains, but this time with small groups of students whom he trained in the critical analysis of all the manifestations of modern society, be they political, cultural, social, or artistic. From 1958 to 1977, Ellul was the president of a juvenile delinquency prevention club as well as playing a very active part in the ecological struggle, particularly within the Committee for the Protection of the Aquitaine Coast.

Note that Troude-Chastenet emphasizes that Ellul's "involvement in the present age *fueled* his writing." It was not only that his reflection and writing influenced the nature and extent of his involvement. Rather, his activism occasioned and informed his writing. Ellul's model of integrating

---

39. Ellul, *Ellul on Religion, Technology, and Politics*, 22.
40. Ibid., 15.

his reflection and action was one of *praxis*, in which there is a mutually constitutive relationship between the two, each shaping the other.

In Ellul's opinion, people—including Christians—have no choice but to be involved with the world.[41] It is both theologically consistent and practically necessary. There is no other option. The only decision to make is *how* one will be involved with the world. Will we be conformed to the patterns of the world? Or will we resist those patterns, instead signifying and symbolizing what the kingdom of God is like? Will our involvement demonstrate hope in our own work? Or hope in the coming kingdom of God, which we do not create or bring, but await? As Troude-Chastenet writes,

> Having decided to turn his back on playing an active part in political life at the beginning of the fourth Republic, Ellul nevertheless continued to incarnate his notion of what a Christian's place was in the world, as far removed from the fundamentalists as the theologians of liberation. Invested with a prophetic mission, the believer, by his thought and action—completely cut off from all the social conformisms—brings in the power of eschatology. This faith in the glorious return of Jesus Christ places the Christian in a revolutionary situation and enables him to face up to all technological dictatorship.[42]

Ellul's prophetic mission in the world, both as a scholar and as an activist, was motivated by faith and hope and modeled after the incarnation. It was involvement that symbolized, in word and in deed, what the kingdom of God is like. It was involvement that was foreign to the world—in the world, but not of it.[43]

Ellul's Continuing Relevance: Exotic Involvement

An important aspect of Ellul's continued relevance is his example of what we would call "exotic involvement." Both as a Christian scholar and as an activist, Ellul was actively involved in the affairs of the world. A well-known scholar whose new works were widely anticipated even when they were not

41. Ellul, "Christian Faith and Social Reality."
42. Ellul, *Ellul on Religion, Technology, and Politics*, 14–15.
43. Ellul's position on the role of Christian action in the world is very closely patterned after that of Karl Barth. For a concise discussion of Barth's position on human action in the world, its relationship to divine action, and its relationship to dialectic, see H. Richard Niebuhr's discussion of "The Kingdom of God and Eschatology in Barth," 120–22.

widely acclaimed, Ellul involved himself in the affairs of scholarship, but not on its terms. As an activist, Ellul involved himself in the affairs of the world, but not on its terms.

"Exotic involvement" captures not only Ellul's approach to scholarship and activism, but also his own position as an outsider and his sense of Christians as foreigners, people not native to the strange land of this world. It suggests an odd or unusual posture toward the world. Ellul's brand of exotic involvement entails allowing God, and not the world, to set the agenda for reflection and action. Ellul, the outsider, was committed to this agenda throughout his career. If there is something about Ellul's pattern of work that is of timeless importance to Christians, it is this pattern of exotic involvement.

In the end, Ellul's own involvement in the world—as a scholar, an activist, a pastor, a municipal civil servant, and a lay leader in the ecumenical movement—was shaped by the commitment articulated in *The Presence of the Kingdom*. Ellul sought always not to be conformed to the patterns of the world, but, rather, to be transformed by the renewing of his mind. As an outsider, Ellul sought to submit to the command to act as a sheep among wolves. He sought in word and in deed to act as a sign of God's covenant and, through his commitment to asking good questions in a dialectical relationship between truth and reality, to shed light upon the modern world.

Key Events in the Life of Jacques Ellul

1912	Born in Bordeaux, France, to Martha Mendes and Joseph Ellul (January 6)
1927	Begins tutoring students in Latin, French, German, and Greek to supplement his family's income
1929	Earns his baccalaureate in the top of his class at Lycee Montaigne
1929	Meets his lifelong best friend, Bernard Charbonneau, at the Protestant Student Federation of the University of Bordeaux
1930	Discovers Karl Marx
1930	Has a "sudden, violent" encounter with God while translating *Faust* (August 10)
1932	Ellul says that by this time his conversion to Christianity is "complete"
1935	Ellul attends "out of curiosity" a Nazi gathering in Munich, Germany
1936	Receives his doctorate at the University of Bordeaux with a thesis titled, "The History and Legal Nature of the Mancipium"
1936	First teaching employment at the University of Montpellier
1937	Married to Yvette Lensvelt
1937–39	Lecturer at University of Strasbourg, from which he is dismissed on political grounds
1940	Birth of his first son, Jean
1941	Birth of his second son, Simon

1942	Ellul's father, Joseph, dies in prison during the German occupation of France
1945	Birth of his third son, Yves
1949	Birth of his daughter, Dominique
1943	Begins to serve as lay pastor of an abandoned church in Martres, with initial services in his dining room
1944	Begins thirty-six-year career at the University of Bordeaux as Professor of the History and Sociology of Institutions in the Faculty of Law, and as Professor in the Institute for Political Studies
1944–45	Serves on the Bordeaux city administration, responsible for public works and commerce
1945–55	Ellul is director of a film club analyzing contemporary cinema
1945–53	Ellul is involved in the foundation and work of the World Council of Churches (WCC)
1947	Ellul's son Simon dies after being hit by a car while running across the street
1950's	Goes by invitation "two or three times a year" to Morocco to give classes in history and courses on the influence of Western law on the Arab world
1951–70	Involved in the National Council of the French Reformed Church
1958–76	President of an organization that works directly with street gangs and "social misfits"
1969	Ellul's close friend Jean Bosc dies
1991	Ellul's wife, Yvette, dies (April 16)
1994	Dies in Pessac, France (May 19)
2001	Jacques Ellul awarded the title "Righteous Among the Nations" by Yad Vashem for his efforts in rescuing Jews during WWII (August 29)

Bibliography

Works by Jacques Ellul

Apocalypse: The Book of Revelation. Translated by George W. Schreiner. New York: Seabury, 1977.
"Christian Faith and Social Reality." In *Sources and Trajectories: Eight Early Articles by Jacques Ellul that Set the Stage*, edited and translated by Marva Dawn, 166-83. Grand Rapids: Eerdmans, 1997.
"Chronicle of the Problems of Civilization: 1. By Way of a Brief Preface." In *Sources and Trajectories: Eight Early Articles by Jacques Ellul that Set the Stage*, edited and translated by Marva Dawn, 10-28. Grand Rapids: Eerdmans, 1997.
The Ethics of Freedom. Edited and translated by Geoffrey W. Bromiley. Grand Rapids: Eerdmans, 1976.
"From Jacques Ellul." In *Introducing Jacques Ellul*, edited and translated by James Y. Holloway, 5-10. Grand Rapids: Eerdmans, 1970.
Histoire des institutions. 5 vols. 6th ed. Paris: Presses universitaires de France, 1982.
Hope in the Time of Abandonment. Translated by C. Edward Hopkin. New York: Seabury, 1973.
"How I Discovered Hope." *The Other Side* 16 (1980) 28-31.
The Humiliation of the Word. Translated by Joyce Main Hanks. Grand Rapids: Eerdmans, 1985.
"Interviews with Jacques Ellul." In David C. Menninger, "Technique and Politics: The Political Thought of Jacques Ellul." PhD diss., University of California Riverside, 1974.
"Jacques Ellul: A Man Who Asks Hard Questions: An Interview with Jacques Ellul by David Gill." *Christianity Today* 28.7 (April 20, 1984) 16-21.
Jacques Ellul on Religion, Technology, and Politics: Conversations with Patrick Troude-Chastenet. Translated by Joan Mendès France. Atlanta: Scholars, 1998. "Karl Barth and Us." *Sojourners* (December 1978) 22-24.
The Meaning of the City. Translated by Dennis Pardee. 1970. Reprint, Eugene, OR: Wipf & Stock, 2011.
Money and Power. Translated by Lavonne Neff. 1984. Reprint, Eugene, OR: Wipf & Stock, 2009.

Bibliography

"Needed: A New Karl Marx!" In *Sources and Trajectories: Eight Early Articles by Jacques Ellul that Set the Stage*, edited and translated by Marva Dawn, 29–38. Grand Rapids: Eerdmans, 1997.

The New Demons. Translated by C. Edward Hopkin. New York: Seabury, 1975.

"On Dialectic." In *Jacques Ellul: Interpretive Essays*, edited and translated by Clifford G. Christians and Jay M. Van Hook, 291–308. Urbana: University of Illinois Press, 1981.

On Freedom, Love, and Power. Compiled, edited, and translated by Willem H. Vanderburg. Toronto: University of Toronto Press, 2010.

Perspectives on Our Age: Jacques Ellul Speaks on His Life and Work. Edited by Willem H. Vanderburg. Translated by Joachim Neugroschel. New York: Seabury, 1981.

The Political Illusion. Translated by Konrad Kellen. New York: Vintage, 1967.

The Politics of God and the Politics of Man. Edited and translated by Geoffrey W. Bromiley. Grand Rapids: Eerdmans, 1972.

Prayer and Modern Man. Translated by C. Edward Hopkin. New York: Seabury, 1970.

The Presence of the Kingdom. Translated by Olive Wyon. 2nd ed. Colorado Springs, CO: Helmers & Howard, 1989.

Propaganda: The Formation of Men's Attitudes. Translated by Konrad Kellen and Jacques Lerner. New York: Vintage, 1973.

The Reason for Being: A Meditation on Ecclesiastes. Translated by Joyce Main Hanks. Grand Rapids: Eerdmans, 1990.

"Response by Jacques Ellul." Translated by Achim Kodderman and Carl Mitcham. *Faith and Freedom* 3.4 (1994) 14–15.

Sources and Trajectories: Eight Early Articles by Jacques Ellul that Set the Stage. Edited and translated by Marva Dawn. Grand Rapids: Eerdmans, 1997.

The Subversion of Christianity. Translated by Geoffrey W. Bromiley. Grand Rapids: Eerdmans, 1986.

"Technique and the Opening Chapters of Genesis." In *Theology and Technology: Essays in Christian Analysis and Exegesis*, edited and translated by Carl Mitcham and Jim Grote, 123–37. Lanham, MD: University Press of America, 1984.

The Technological Society. Translated by John Wilkinson. New York: Vintage, 1964.

"The Situation in Europe." In *The Church and the Disorder of Society: An Ecumenical Study*, edited by Willem Adolph Visser 't Hooft, 50–61. London: SCM, 1948.

"The Technological Order." *Technology and Culture* 3 (1962) 394–421.

To Will and to Do: An Ethical Research for Christians. Translated by C. Edward Hopkin. Philadelphia: Pilgrim, 1969.

"With a View Toward Assessing the Facts." *The New York Times*, July 1, 1973, 13E.

Other Works Cited

Allison, Gregg R. "Theological Interpretation of Scripture: An Introduction and Preliminary Evaluation." *Southern Baptist Journal of Theology* 14 (2010) 28–36.

American Psychological Association. "DSM-5 Development." Online: http://www.dsm5.org/Pages/Default.aspx.

Augustine. *City of God*. New York: Penguin, 2010.

Bailey, Lloyd R. Review of *The Judgment of Jonah*, by Jacques Ellul. *Duke Divinity School Review* 37 (1972) 172–74.

Billings, J. Todd. *The Word of God for the People of God: An Entryway to the Theological Interpretation of Scripture*. Grand Rapids: Eerdmans, 2010.
Boneu, E. J. Review of *Propagandes*, by Jacques Ellul. *Revista Española de la opinion publica* 1 (1963) 338–39.
Bonhoeffer, Dietrich. *Creation and Fall: A Theological Exposition of Genesis 1–3*. Edited and translated by Martin Rüter et al. Dietrich Bonhoeffer Works 3. Minneapolis: Fortress, 1997.
Broker Outpost. "Patriot Act." Online: http://www.brokeroutpost.com/reference/23676.htm.
Bromiley, Geoffrey W. "Barth's Influence on Jacques Ellul." In *Jacques Ellul: Interpretive Essays*, edited by Clifford G. Christians and Jay M. Van Hook, 32–51. Urbana: University of Illinois Press, 1981.
———. "Editor's Preface." In Jacques Ellul, *The Ethics of Freedom*, edited and translated by Geoffrey W. Bromiley, 5. Grand Rapids: Eerdmans, 1976.
———. "Translator's Preface." In Jacques Ellul, *The Judgment of Jonah*, 5–8. Grand Rapids: Eerdmans, 1971.
Brzezinski, Zbigniew. *Between Two Ages: America's Role in the Technetronic Era*. New York: Viking, 1970.
Childs, Brevard. *Old Testament Books for Pastor and Teacher*. Philadelphia: Westminster, 1977.
Christians, Clifford G., and Jay M. Van Hook. *Jacques Ellul: Interpretive Essays*. Urbana: University of Illinois Press, 1981.
Chua, Amy. *World on Fire: How Exporting Free Market Democracy Breeds Ethnic Hatred and Global Instability*. New York: Doubleday, 2003.
Clendenin, Daniel B. *Theological Method in Jacques Ellul*. Lanham, MD: University Press of America, 1987.
CNet. "Email 'n Walk—As Seen on the BBC—for iPhone." Online: http://download.cnet.com/Email-n-Walk-As-seen-on-the-BBC/3000-2094_4-10914844.html.
Cole, Deborah. "Fukushima Fallout: Germany Abandons Nuclear Energy." *Sydney Morning Herald*, May 31, 2011. Online: http://www.smh.com.au/world/fukushima-fallout-germany-abandons-nuclear-energy-20110530-1fczb.html.
Columbia Encyclopedia, 6th ed., s.v. "Fascism." May 24, 2011. Online: http://www.encyclopedia.com/doc/1E1-fascism.html/.
Cox, Harvey Gallagher. Review of *The Meaning of the City*, by Jacques Ellul. *Commonweal* (July 9, 1971) 351–57.
———. *The Secular City: Secularization and Urbanization in Theological Perspective*. New York: Collier, 1990.
Dauvergne, Peter. "Automobiles." In *The Shadows of Consumption: Consequences for the Global Environment*, 33–64. Cambridge: MIT Press, 2008.
Dear, I. C. B., and M. R. D. Foot. "Fascism." In *The Oxford Companion to World War II*. New York: Oxford University Press, 2001. Online: http://www.encyclopedia.com/doc/10129-fascism.html/.
Falk, Howard. Review of *The Technological Society*, by Jacques Ellul. *Technology and Culture* 6 (1965) 532–35.
Fasching, Darrell J. *The Thought of Jacques Ellul: A Systematic Exposition*. Lewiston, NY: Edwin Mellen, 1981.
Fletcher, Joseph. *Situation Ethics: The New Morality*. Philadelphia: Westminster, 1966.
Fowl, Stephen. *Theological Interpretation of Scripture*. Eugene, OR: Cascade Books, 2009.

Bibliography

Fox News. "Texting Teen Falls Down Open Manhole." July 11, 2009. Online: http://www.foxnews.com/story/0,2933,531684,00.html.
Fukuyama, Francis. *Our Posthuman Future: Consequences of the Biotechnology Revolution.* New York: Picador, 2003.
———. "The World's Most Dangerous Ideas: Transhumanism." *Foreign Policy* (144) 42–43.
Garrigou-Lagrange, Madeleine. *In Season, Out of Season: An Introduction to the Thought of Jacques Ellul.* Translated by Lani K. Niles. San Francisco: Harper & Row, 1982.
Gill, David W. "Jacques Ellul and Francis Schaeffer: Two Views of Western Civilization." *Fides et Historia* 13 (1981) 23–37.
———. *The Word of God in the Ethics of Jacques Ellul.* Metuchen, NJ: Scarecrow, 1984.
Ginsberg, Allen. "Howl." In *Howl, and Other Poems.* San Franscisco: City Lights, 1956.
Glaeser, Edward. *Triumph of the City: How Our Greatest Invention Makes Us Richer, Smarter, Greener, Healthier, and Happier.* New York: Penguin, 2011.
Goddard, Andrew. "Jacques Ellul on Idolatry." In *Idolatry: False Worship in the Bible, Early Judaism and Christianity*, edited Stephen C. Barton, 228–45. London: T. & T. Clark, 2007.
———. *Living the Word, Resisting the World: The Life and Thought of Jacques Ellul.* Waynesboro, GA: Paternoster, 2002.
———. "Obituary: Jacques Ellul." *Studies in Christian Ethics* 9 (1996) 140–153.
Gorringe, T. J. *A Theology of the Built Environment: Justice, Empowerment, Redemption.* New York: Cambridge University Press, 2002.
Grossman, Lev. "Mark Zuckerberg." *Time,* December 15, 2010. Online: http://www.time.com/time/specials/packages/printout/0,29239,2036683_2037183_2037185,00.html.
Hadden, Jeffrey K. "Is God a Country Boy?" Review of *The Meaning of the City*, by Jacques Ellul. *Journal for the Scientific Study of Religion* 12 (1973) 120–21.
Hanks, Joyce Main. *Jacques Ellul: An Annotated Bibliography of Primary Works.* Stamford, CT: JAI, 2000.
———. "The Politics of God and the Politics of Ellul." *Journal of the Evangelical Theological Society* 35 (1992) 217–30.
Harvey, David. *A Companion to Marx's Capital.* New York: Verso, 2010.
Helmore, Edward. "US Air Force Prepares Drones to End Era of Fighter Pilots." *The Guardian,* August 22, 2009. Online: http://www.guardian.co.uk/world/2009/aug/22/us-air-force-drones-pilots-afghanistan?INTCMP=ILCNETTXT3487/.
Herman, Edward S., and Noam Chomsky. *Manufacturing Consent: The Political Economy of the Mass Media.* New York: Pantheon, 1988.
Hitler, Adolf. *Mein Kampf.* Translated by Ralph Manheim. 1925. Reprint, Boston: Houghton Mifflin, 1971.
Holloway, James Y. *Introducing Jacques Ellul.* Grand Rapids: Eerdmans, 1970.
Howard, Ebenezer. *Garden Cities of To-Morrow.* Cambridge: MIT Press, 1965.
Huxley, Aldous. *A Brave New World Revisited.* San Francisco: Harper, 1998.
Jacobs, Jane. *The Death and Life of Great American Cities.* 50th anniversary ed. New York: Modern Library, 2011.
Johnson, Keith L. "Depravity and Hope in the City: Karl Barth in Conversation with *The Wire*." In *Corners in the City of God: Theology and* The Wire, edited by Jonathan Tran and Myles Werntz. Eugene, OR: Cascade, forthcoming.
Kasarda, John, and Greg D. Lindsay. *Aerotropolis: How We'll Live Next.* New York: Farrar, Strauss & Giroux, 2010.

Bibliography

Koike, Robert. "Hiroshima Mayor Blasts Fukushima Handling, Demands Energy Rethink." Majirox News, August 6, 2011. Online: http://www.majiroxnews.com/2011/08/06/hiroshima-mayor-blasts-fukushima-handling-demands-energy-re-think.

Kraemer, Hendrik. *Theology of the Laity*. Philadelphia: Westminster, 1958.

Lang, Fritz. *Metropolis*. Berlin: UFA, 1927.

Le Corbusier. *The City of To-Morrow and Its Planning*. Mineola, NY: Dover, 1987.

Lerner, Daniel. Review of *Propagandes*, by Jacques Ellul. *American Sociological Review* 29 (1963) 793–94.

Lifton, Robert Jay. *Death in Life: Survivors of Hiroshima*. New York: Random House, 1968.

Lovekin, David. *Technique, Discourse, and Consciousness: An Introduction to the Philosophy of Jacques Ellul*. Bethlehem, PA: Lehigh University Press, 1991.

Mander, Jerry. *The Case against the Global Economy: And for a Turn to the Local*. San Francisco: Sierra Club, 1996.

Marty, Martin. "Introduction: Creative Misuses of Jacques Ellul." In *Jacques Ellul: Interpretive Essays*, edited by Clifford G. Christians and Jay M. Van Hook, 3–13. Urbana: University of Illinois Press, 1981.

Marx, Karl. *Capital: A Critique of Political Economy*. 3 vols. New York: Penguin, 1992–1993.

———. *The Communist Manifesto*. New York: Oxford University Press, 2008.

———. *Grundrisse: Foundations of the Critique of Political Economy*. New York: Penguin, 1993.

McLuhan, Marshall. *Understanding Media: The Transformations of Man*. New York: McGraw-Hill, 1964.

McNeill, William. "Cities and Their Consequences." *The American Interest* 2.4 (2007) 5–12.

Meggs, Philip B., and Alston W. Purvis. *Meggs' History of Graphic Design*. 4th ed. Hoboken, NJ: Wiley, 2006.

Menninger, David C. "Politics or Technique? A Defense of Jacques Ellul." *Polity* 14 (1981) 110–27.

———. "Technique and Politics: The Political Thought of Jacques Ellul." PhD diss., University of California Riverside, 1974.

Merton, Robert K. Foreword to *The Technological Society*, by Jacques Ellul. New York: Vintage, 1964.

Merton, Thomas. Review of *The Technological Society*, by Jacques Ellul. *Commonweal*, December 4, 1964, 385.

Mill, John Stuart. "On the Definition of Political Economy; And on the Method of Investigation Proper to It." In *Essays on Some Unsettled Questions*, 120–64. Rev. ed. London: Parker & Strand, 1844.

Mounier, Emmanuel. *A Personalist Manifesto*. New York: Longmans, Green, 1938.

Mumford, Lewis. "Authoritarian and Democratic Technics." *Technology and Culture* 5 (1964) 1–8.

———. *The City in History: Its Origins, Its Transformations, and Its Prospects*. New York: Mariner, 1968.

Niebuhr, H. Richard. "The Kingdom of God and Eschatology in Barth." In *Theology, History, and Culture: Major Unpublished Writings*, edited by William Stacy Johnson. New Haven: Yale University Press, 1996.

Newbigin, Lesslie. *Foolishness to the Greeks: The Gospel and Western Culture*. Grand Rapids: Eerdmans, 1986.

Bibliography

The Onion. "CIA's 'Facebook' Program Dramatically Cut Agency's Costs." March 21, 2011. Online: http://www.theonion.com/video/cias-facebook-program-dramatically-cut-agencys-cos,19753/.

Owen, David. *Green Metropolis: Why Living Smaller, Living Closer, and Driving Less Are the Keys to Sustainability.* New York: Riverhead, 2009.

Postman, Neil. *Amusing Ourselves to Death: Public Discourse in the Age of Show Business.* New York: Viking, 1985.

―――. *Crazy Talk, Stupid Talk: How We Defeat Ourselves by the Way We Talk and What to Do about It.* New York: Viking, 1976.

―――. *The Disappearance of Childhood.* New York: Vintage, 1982.

―――. Public address. Madison, WI, November 24, 1968.

―――. "Science and the Story We Need." *First Things* 69 (1997) 29–32.

―――. *Technopoly: The Surrender of Culture to Technology.* New York: Knopf, 1992.

Radiation Effects Research Foundation. "Frequently Asked Questions." Online: http://www.rerf.or.jp/general/qa_e/qa1.html.

Ritzer, George. *The McDonaldization of Society: An Investigation into the Changing Character of Contemporary Social Life.* Newbury Park, CA: Pine Forge, 1993.

Schaeffer, Francis A. *Death in the City.* Downers Grove, IL: InterVarsity, 1969.

Singer, Peter. *Marx: A Very Short Introduction.* New York: Oxford University Press, 2001.

Spinks, D. Christopher. *The Bible and the Crisis of Meaning: Debates on the Theological Interpretation of Scripture.* London: T. & T. Clark, 2007.

Streitfield, David. "Pentagon Seeks a Few Good Social Networkers." August 2, 2011. Online: http://bits.blogs.nytimes.com/2011/08/02/pentagon-seeks-social-networking-experts/?smid=tw-nytimesbits&seid=auto/.

Talmadge, Eric. "First 24 Hours Shaped Japan Nuke Crisis." Associated Press, July 1, 2011. Online: http://www.usatoday.com/money/topstories/2011-07-02-3872181737_x.htm.

Taylor, Frederick Winslow. *The Principles of Scientific Management.* New York: Harper, 1911.

Terlizzese, Lawrence. *Hope in the Thought of Jacques Ellul.* Eugene, OR: Cascade, 2004.

Tillich, Paul. *Systematic Theology.* Vol. 1, *Reason and Revelation, Being and God.* Chicago: University of Chicago Press, 1951.

Toffler, Alvin. *Future Shock.* New York: Random House, 1970.

Tran, Jonathan, and Myles Werntz, editors. *Corners in the City of God: Theology and the Wire.* Eugene, OR: Cascade, forthcoming.

Treier, Daniel J. *Introducing Theological Interpretation of Scripture: Recovering a Christian Practice.* Grand Rapids: Baker, 2008.

―――. "Typology." In *Dictionary for Theological Interpretation of the Bible*, edited by Kevin J. Vanhoozer et al., 823–27. Grand Rapids: Baker, 2005.

Tye, Larry. *The Father of Spin: Edward L. Bernays and the Birth of Public Relations.* New York: Henry Holt, 1998.

Vahanian, Gabriel. Review of *Le bluff technologique*, by Jacques Ellul. *The Ellul Studies Bulletin* (August 1988) 11.

van Boekel, Jan. *The Betrayal by Technology: A Portrait of Jacques Ellul.* Amsterdam, ReRun Productions, 1992. Film. English transcript online: http://www.archive.org/details/JacquesEllul-TheBetrayalByTechnology-EnglishTranscript.

Vance, Rupert B. Review of *The Technological Society*, by Jacques Ellul. *Social Forces* 46 (1968) 416–17.

Vanhoozer, Kevin J. "Introduction." In *Dictionary for Theological Interpretation of the Bible*, edited by Kevin J. Vanhoozer et al., 19–26. Grand Rapids: Baker, 2005.

Wang, David. "Ellul on New Urbanism." *Christian Scholar's Review* 38 (2009) 457–70.

Webster, John B. "Editorial." *International Journal of Systematic Theology* 12 (2010) 116–17.

Wilkinson, John. "Introduction." In Jacques Ellul, *The Meaning of the City*. Translated by Dennis Pardee. Grand Rapids: Eerdmans, 1970.

———. "Translator's Introduction." In Jacques Ellul, *The Technological Society*, ix–xx. New York: Vintage, 1964.

Winter, Gibson. Review of *The Meaning of the City* and *Prayer and Modern Man*, by Jacques Ellul. *Journal of the American Academy of Religion* 40 (1972) 118–22.

Winter, Rhonda. "Switzerland Abandons Nuclear Power." May 26, 2011. Online: http://cleantechnica.com/2011/05/26/nuclear-power-no-more-in-switzerland/.

Yabokov, Alexey, et al. "Chernobyl: Consequences of the Catastrophe for People and the Environment." *Annals of the New York Academy of Sciences* 1181 (2009) 1–327.

What Is Google+ and Do I Need It? [Video]. Online: http://www.youtube.com/watch?v=hC_M6PzXS9g/.

Index

Activism, 13, 76, 160
Adam, 48, 68, 70, 105
Antinomianism, 131
Apocalypse, 114–15, 117,
Apocalyptic, 74–76
Apostle Paul, 4, 13, 35, 131, 135, 144, 157
Augustine, 57, 62, 136
Automobile, 31–34

Babel, 70
Babylon, 70, 75
Barth, Karl, 6, 10–11, 12, 35, 58, 83, 99, 101, 122, 135, 142, 155, 159
Bernays, Edward, 39
Bonhoeffer, Dietrich, 94n28, 101
Bordeaux, 1, 7–8, 64
Bosc, Jean, 5, 6
Bromiley, Geoffry, 106, 148

Cain, 68—69, 74, 78
Calvin, John, 10, 12, 48
Capitalism, 4, 8, 31, 81–84, 86–88, 90–92,
Charbonneau, Bernard, 5–6, 89
Christian life,
    as agonistic tension, 123, 134
    demands of, 140–41
    and freedom, 133–38
    and responsibility, 138–39
Christianity, 2, 8
    American, 62
    anti-religious, 35
    Christian ethics, 121–24, 127–44
    de-Christianization, 45–46
    Ellul's conversion to, 3–4, 12, 83
    in the world, 13–18, 36, 44–46, 56, 58, 64, 72–76, 81, 87–88, 96–97, 100–101, 159–60
Intellectual life/scholarship, 9, 10, 12, 59, 119–20, 151, 153, 158
Protestantism, 2, 48
Reformed Church, 6, 9, 12, 48, 158
National Council of the French Reformed Church, 9
Roman Catholic Church, 8, 12, 63
Christians, Clifford, 147
Church, 8–9, 12, 13–14, 18, 101, 108
    and ethics, 132, 138–40, 143–44
    and politics, 96–97
    propaganda in the, 38–39, 43–46
    and scripture, 108, 119–20
    societal role of the, 140
    task of the, 73
City,
    and economic growth, 61, 78
    global connectedness of, 77
    growth of the, 61, 77
    Scriptural reality of the, 74
    transformation of the, 70–71
Cold War, 21, 81, 82, 86
Communication, 17, 38, 46–48, 58, 59
Computer, 25, 57, 58
Correlation, 151–54, 156
    Cox, Harvey, 62, 63, 94
Creation, 47, 67–68
    narrative of, 101–6
    See also New Creation

Index

Dehumanization, 15, 18, 20, 35, 38, 40, 57, 87, 88, 121, 124
Democracy, 31, 81–82, 86, 90
Desacralization, 95–96
Dialectic, 35, 51, 83, 117, 151–52, 156–58

Ecclesiastes, 38, 76n, 109–14, 116, 119
Ecclesiology, 143–44
   ecclesiastical involvement, 8–9
Economics
   Politics and, 81–97
   Marxism and, 4–5, 37
   as subdivision of technique, 22–23
   growth related to urbanism, 61, 78
Eden, 68, 104–5
Education
   Ellul's, 2–3
   images in, 54
Efficiency, 16, 18, 22, 23, 25, 29, 38, 105, 124, 127
Ellul (family)
   Dominique (daughter), 6, 162
   Jean (son), 6, 161
   Joseph (father), 1, 161, 162
   Martha (mother), 1, 161
   Simon (son), 6, 34, 161, 162
   Yves (son), 6, 123, 162
   Yvette (wife), 6, 34, 86, 161, 162
Entertainment, 42, 90
Ethics, 121–45
   in Ellul's work, 121
   and freedom, 131
   and morality, 132
   nature of, 127
   pertaining to God's will, 128
   purpose of, 122
   situational, 137
   and technology, 124

Facts, 21, 49–50, 53
   and reductionism, 24
   in propaganda, 41–42
   understanding through Christianity, 13–14
Faith, 10–11, 47–48, 53, 56, 118, 123–24, 131
   integration with learning, 18, 150, 154–55
   vs. religion, 35
   in technique, 94
Fasching, Darrell, 20, 117
Fascism, 85–86,
   explanation of 85
   Ellul's opinion of, 85–86
   Nazi gathering in Munich (1935), 7, 39, 85
Faust, 3, 90
Film, 42, 49
France, 1, 2, 3, 6, 19, 150
   war in, 7, 81, 85
Free will, 34, 103
Freedom, 15, 26, 30, 31, 35–36, 40, 42, 75–76, 78, 86, 95–97, 103–4, 121, 122, 131–44
   nature of, 134

Gill, David, vii, 58, 59, 147
Goddard, Andrew, 1
Goebbels, Joseph, 39
Gorringe, Timothy, 71, 75–77
Government, 67
   Ellul's service in, 76, 9, 8, 158
   and propaganda, 43

Hanks, Joyce Main, 95
Heidegger, Martin, 19
Hitler, Adolf, 39, 89
Holy Spirit, 14–15, 119, 136, 140,
   in Christian character, 142–43
   in Christian ethics, 127
Hope, 123, 159
   for city, 70–72
   despite idolatry of image, 56
   despite technology, 34–36
   in Ellul's writing, 153, 157
   in ethics, 123
   faith as source of, 18, 35
   in Revelation, 118

Idolatry, 48
   of images, 56–57
   in politics, 94–95
   resistance to, 56–58
Image (vs. word), 49–52

Index

resisting idolatry of the image, 55–59
Imago Dei, 103
Individualism, 40, 137, 143
Indivisibility (of technique), 27–28, 33
Industrialism, 61–62
Industry, 19, 38, 105

Jacobs, Jane, 61, 63
Jerusalem, 7, 71–71, 81
   New Jerusalem, 64, 71–72, 75n, 117
   church in, 144
Jesus Christ, 11–18, 36, 43,–47, 60, 71–72, , 98,
   and freedom, 132, 136
   as hermenuetical approach, 119
   as incarnate word, 99
Justification, 92–94

Kingdom of God, 16, 73–74, 75, 117, 159

Language, 47–46, 52, 54, 58
Law, 67
   moral, 131
   natural, 128, 155
   study of, 2–3, 7, 150–151, 162
   teaching, 9, 11, 162
Laypeople, 9, 12, 14, 110, 138, 140, 142, 143
Le Corbusier, 61, 74–75

Machines, 19–20, 25, 36, 38, 56, 62, 78, 94,
Marx, Karl, 3–5, 9, 10, 11, 22, 36, 55, 82, 83, 84, 87, 88, 153, 157
Materialism, 5, 54
McLuhan, Marshall, 27, 32
Media, 20, 27n, 38, 40–41, 59
Money, 87, 93,
   Ellul's view on, 89–92
   and idolatry, 94
   and necessity, 89–91
   and power, 86–88,
Moralism, 130—132
Morality,
   and ethics, 132
   freedom from, 132
   and God's revelation, 130

   independent from God, 128
   and technique, 29, 124–27
Mounier, Emmanuel, 8
Mumford, Lewis, 19, 61–63, 71, 75, 79, 90–91
Municipal government,
   Ellul's experience in, 7–8, 76, 158

Necessity,
   of money, 89–92
   of technique, 124
Neo-orthodox, 64
New creation, 70–74, 96, 117, 153
   See also, Creation
Nuclear,
   energy, 27–28
   weapons, 21, 82

Obedience, 134
Orthodoxy, 39, 41
Orthopraxis, 41

Paul, the Apostle. *See* Apostle Paul
Personalist Movement, 8
Politics,
   Christian response to, 58, 140–141
   and economics, 81–97
   Ellul in, 12, 158
   of freedom, 95–96
   of God, 96–97
   and resistance, 6
Postman, Neil, ix$n1$, 31n45, 36n55
Poverty, 2, 5, 9, 12, 82, 136–37, 144
Progress, 16, 26–27, 37, 66, 87, 118, 155, 157
Propaganda, 23, 38–59, 82, 139
   political, 42
   purpose of, 40–42
   and reality, 41
   sociological, 42
   spiritual effects of, 43–46
   types and features of, 42–43

Qohelet, 109–13
Questions, 58, 142–50, 153–56

Reality,
   and propaganda, 41

Index

vs. Truth, 53–55, 113–15, 153
Resistance, 21, 35,
   to idolatry, 56–58
   to dehumanization, 121
   to Nazi occupation of France, 6–8, 81, 86
Revolution, 5, 15–16, 17, 82–83

Satan, 14, 75, 96, 124
Scholarship, 12, 13, 18, 98
   Biblical, 100, 110, 115, 116
   Christian, 119–20
   Ellul as a Christian Scholar, 10, 145–60
Science, 31, 53–54, 57–58, 80, 83,
   human sciences, 65–67, 80
Scripture, 11, 47–48, 64–71, 98–122, 131–34,
   as revelation 101
   Ellul's understanding of, 98–101
Socialism, 31, 82, 86–88, 91–92,
   and capitalism, 86
   and technique, 91–92
   Ellul's response to, 84, 87–88
Spanish Civil War, 6–7, 86
Speech, 46–47, 51–52, 54, 58
State, the, 15, 31, 84–85, 87, 88, 89, 92, 95, 122, 130, 140,
Stringfellow, William, 63

Taylor, Frederick Winslow, 25, 29, 32
Technics, 15, 16, 17, 18
Technique, 24–29
   artificiality of, 32
   autonomy of, 29, 33–34
   and Eden, 105
   and faith, 94
   monism in, 27–28, 33

   and morality, 29, 124
   necessity of, 124
   rationality of, 31
   and socialism, 91–92
   subdivision of, 22–23
   and virtues, 126
   and work, 91
Technological society, 21–24, 29, 30–31, 36–37, 38, 40–42, 49, 51, 63, 83–84
   morality in, 124–27
Television, 20, 42, 49, 52, 53
Theological interpretation, 98–119
Tillich, Paul, 152–54
Totalitarianism, 89, 92
   Society in, 36
Troude-Chastenet, Patrick, 89, 155–56, 158–59
Truth
   eschatological, 56
   and propaganda, 38–45
   vs. Reality, 53–55, 113–15, 153 Scripture as, 100, 108

Word, 46–59
   vs. image, 49–53
Work, 91–95,
World War II, 15, 39, 60, 81
   Free French zone, 7
   the French resistance, 81, 6–8
   German occupation, 81, 85
   Holocaust, 7, 81
   Nazism, 7, 16, 59
   Propaganda during, 39

Yad Vashem, 7, 81
   and Ellul's designation as "Righteous Among the Nations," 7, 81

www.ingramcontent.com/pod-product-compliance
Lightning Source LLC
Chambersburg PA
CBHW030112170426
43198CB00009B/588